THE

UNMASKING

GREAT

THE LIES

DECEIVER

OF SATAN

KENNETH COPLEY

MOODY PRESS

CHICAGO

All Scripture quotations, unless otherwise indicated, are taken from the *New King James Version.* Copyright © 1982 by Thomas Nelson, Inc. Used by permission. All rights reserved.

Scripture quotations marked KJV are taken from the King James Version.

Library of Congress Cataloging-in-Publication Data

Copley, Kenneth.
   The great deceiver / Kenneth Copley.
    p. cm.
   ISBN 0-8024-8593-6
   1. Spiritual warfare. 2. Devil. I. Title.

BV4509.5 .C675 2001
235´.4--dc21

00-068971

1 3 5 7 9 10 8 6 4 2

Printed in the United States of America

To my loving wife, Elizabeth,
precious wife of my youth
and caring mother of our children.
You have greatly enriched my life.

ACKNOWLEDGMENTS

Effective counseling requires that each counselee be assured that the counselor will treat all that is shared with a most strict degree of confidentiality. When the counselor ministers as a representative of our Lord Jesus Christ, the integrity of confidentiality is lifted to its highest elevation. Readers of this book will become immediately aware of my use of examples derived from stories out of the lives of numerous friends and counselees. Our Lord's earthly ministry demonstrated that truth from the Word of God becomes fresh and understandable when viewed in real-life situations. Although I have exercised the utmost care in the assignment of gender and place to protect each from being identified, I want to salute each person who graciously granted me permission to use his or her story. Because each has counted the protection of their privacy of less importance than the exalting of biblical truth, they have agreed to tell their stories. For that I am deeply appreciative, and I express my profound gratititude.

I am also deeply grateful to my dear family for their support during the writing of this book. Although for a time they felt like the widowed and fatherless, they stayed with me and offered their undiminished support. They are a wonderful gift from God.

CONTENTS

FOREWORD

Some people write about a subject that interests them, but others write from life experiences. This book is written from a man's life experience. Let me explain this to you.

A number of years ago I got a call from the wife of a man who had been very skeptical about the whole issue of spiritual warfare. But when a member of your own family exhibits behavior that you know in your heart and spirit is not normal, nor is it psychological but a spiritual warfare issue, you cry out to God and seek counsel. "What do I do now?" this woman asked. In time I was able to share some steps of action to free this family member.

This was Ken Copley's baptism into spiritual warfare. Though a pastor, he was experiencing spiritual warfare and agreed to see me for counsel. He began to apply the information that I gave him and he saw God set his son free.

God began to direct others his way to share with them what he was learning from the study of Scripture and life's experiences. Now, years later after ministering to thousands in conferences and personal counseling, his rich experiences and years of Bible study have been set down in this book.

May you be blessed and encouraged in the spiritual battles of life as you journey through this excellent book by a close personal friend, Dr. Ken Copley.

JIM LOGAN
Author, *Reclaiming Surrendered Ground*

EXPOSING
THE LIES

For many Christians, spiritual warfare is an offbeat or even "weird" subject. Some believers do not even accept the idea that Satan, or his demons, exist, or that they possess any power to attack and afflict us in this age.

For a long time, I maintained that very mind-set, oblivious to the reality of an active Satan and scorning those who posed the whole spiritual warfare scenario. Then one day my oldest son experienced his own personal and harrowing battle with the enemy. What happened annihilated any misgivings I had about such warfare, as my whole family was suddenly plunged into a heart-wringing and soul-disturbing situation that nearly took my son away. I asked, "How could this be happening to my son, my family? Didn't God keep Satan away from us? Didn't He prevent Satan from influencing or touching His children?"

What followed was a battle unlike anything I'd ever imagined in nonfiction or even fiction. I rejoice about that today, because that incident opened up whole vistas of hope and healing to those engaging the enemy and not knowing it. Now I can help people deeply entrenched in the enemy's lies and trickery. Until my son's problem, I was often forced into the old clichés people use when Christians with problems came to me and I couldn't seem to help them resolve them. Old standards like "You don't have enough faith," or "Just read your Bible daily and you will get beyond this."

I have learned that such responses are often the very lies Satan himself wants to foist on us. Don't get me wrong. I believe God is all-powerful, loving, and intimately involved in our lives. The enemy has no power that can stymie Him, or even derail His plans.

That does not mean, though, that God's world is not a battleground, or that Satan cannot influence and even attack believers. During my son's time of crisis, a gracious friend patiently showed me step-by-step what this biblical battle involves and how to win it. Ultimately, my son gained true freedom in Christ. And I discovered in no uncertain terms that our common enemy "walks about like a roaring lion, seeking whom he may devour" (1 Peter 5:8). That lion stalks all of us at different times and in different ways. But his goal remains the same: to devour us.

For seventeen years I served as senior pastor of three churches. During this time I gave little attention to spiritual warfare because I thought only "crazy, radical kooks" were involved in it. This changed after my son came to freedom and I began to witness the real destruction and havoc Satan wreaks in the lives of Christians and others.

As news of our family's struggle got out through the grapevine, my phone rang constantly, not because people were critical of me or my son; but people with desperate needs wanted help and believed my experience might offer them the insight they needed. As these beleaguered folks told me their stories, I began to research and understand the field of spiritual warfare and saw it not only as a personal struggle that a few Christians experience because of dabbling in the occult or other practices, but as a worldwide battle Satan wages for every heart and mind. I realized this was not unusual or abnormal, but rather the very thing all of us must deal with daily.

Please understand from the start that spiritual warfare is not about attacking the devil. No swordsman, no matter how skilled, would consider going up against a dragon with billions of demons at his right and left. Christ is the One who has attacked, stopped, and broken Satan. It's not even up to us to knock him down a peg or two for divine spite.

No, what warfare is about, in essence, is exposing the lies Satan uses in lives through showing people God's truth. Satan's primary weapons are lies and deception—twisting, negating, and turning around the truth of God in any way he can to gain an advantage. My job is to help expose these schemes in a counselee's life. As Satan's lies are etched clearly against the prism of truth, they're exposed, and freedom and healing result. A whole new sense of hope and expectation grasps their hearts and personalities. Where there was struggle, despair, and (in some cases) a desire to end it all, a new exuberance appears and Jesus becomes a central figure in everything they do.

That is my goal for everyone I counsel and for you who read this book. My purpose is to expose the thinking and falsehoods of the enemy, break their power over a person's life, and thus set him or her free.

Each part of the book concludes with "Beyond the Deceptions," a set of questions to help evaluate where you are in recognizing and using God's truth in the daily spiritual battle.

All stories in the book are based on authentic counseling experiences. The names have been chaned to protect the privacy of individuals, but the case studies are actual.

If you find yourself in a struggle to read the Scriptures or pray, resist sin, forgive an offense, or change an attitude, I guarantee you are involved in spiritual warfare. If God's love and power in your life seem distant and you struggle to draw closer to the heavenly Father, a spiritual battle is underway. It's those ensnared in such circumstances whom I want to help. Believe me, I know what it's like to live in terror of tomorrow. My son's experience almost destroyed our whole family.

But through Christ all things are possible. He preserved me, and He will do the same for you—if you seek Him and depend on Him for truth, hope, and power.

WE HAVE
AN ENEMY

THE GREAT DECEPTION... AND THE TRUTH

SATAN'S LIE: "I am not your enemy."
(See 2 Corinthians 11:14.)

GOD'S TRUTH: *"Be sober, be vigilant; because your adversary the devil walks about like a roaring lion"* (1 Peter 5:8).

CHAPTER ONE

SPIRITUAL WARFARE: A CASE HISTORY

A psychiatrist sent Mary to me. As we talked, I saw a despondent woman with a deep sense of failure and low self-esteem. I quickly learned she took a heavy dose of Thorazine every four hours to control an inner rage that churned inside like molten lava in a ready-to-erupt volcano. Her family was often subjected to outbursts neither she nor they understood. Her doctor sent her to me because he thought I could help her solve the root problems that drove the rage.

Though I always try to be compassionate and understanding with people who hurt deeply, I also am fairly straightforward about exposing the crux of the issue. There is little point in dancing around the subject when a direct question can lay out the real problem. Thus, I chose to plunge in and ask Mary what she was angry about.

Her blunt answer made me gasp. She said, "My stepfather. My mother married him when I was three years old. My mother worked nights. Shortly after their marriage, he began to molest me."

As she revealed more of the history, Mary clearly showed me she had suffered greatly at the hands of this man. At such times as a counselor, one wishes he had the power of the courts and the justice system to deal with people like this stepfather. But all I had was Mary and her broken heart. I probed more and suddenly she exclaimed, tears in her eyes, "When I was a teenager, he raped me many times."

Sometimes barely able to speak, so emotional was this conversation, I finally let her talk with only minor interruptions and questions. That's often the best way to help such people. She concluded, "I am a believer in Christ, but I still want to kill my stepfather. The only thing that keeps me from blowing his head off with a shotgun is my seven-year-old daughter. If I murdered my stepfather, my daughter, who is fatherless, would go into foster care and likely suffer the same kind of abuse I have suffered."

As Mary talked, I began to get a picture of the real problem that gripped her. She was believing a lie that Satan often uses in such circumstances, a lie that usually leaves the soul bankrupt and the heart deeply wounded. She believed that her stepfather had destroyed her life.

Mary reinforced that insight when she told me, "I feel dirty, trapped, worthless."

Because of what her stepfather had done to her in word and in deed, he had made her feel not only that she wanted what he had done, but that she had also deserved it. But even this did not satisfy him as he repeatedly pounded into her the idea that she was worthless and useless and would never do any better in life if she didn't let him continue his assaults. He became the mouthpiece of Satan as he subjected her to more lies about her value as a person and her potential as a woman. The result was a desperate need for affirmation, which he was only too glad to give in the form of more abuse.

THE NATURE OF THE WARFARE

This woman was definitely involved in spiritual warfare. The primary battle was not emotional but spiritual, for Satan was using her stepfather to give lies about her person, lies about her great worth as God's created and loved child. Yet Mary's spiritual battle may not be obvious to readers; the enemy is subtle. He does not like to reveal himself frontally if he can come in a back door and conk you over the head without you realizing who did it.

In this case, Satan had attacked Mary through many means. First, he had incited her stepfather against her. Second, he made her fear telling the truth. Third, by various lies he had enslaved Mary to her past and made her unable to let go of it and thus find freedom.

As a counselor, I could not change her past or her stepfather. But I could help her take back the ground she had lost. That meant dealing with her present feelings of anger and worthlessness. Such feelings—of brokenness, of uselessness, and of being tainted and rejected by God—are probably the chief ways Satan destroys Christians today. We cannot change the past, and the past so influences our present that we find real living impossible.

This is the essence of spiritual warfare. It's not some hyperventilated idea of demon possession where a person's head revolves 360 degrees à la *The Exorcist*. Rather, it's the subtle, day-by-day feeding of lies into our minds, which we begin to believe and finally swallow wholesale, locking us off from a closer relationship with Christ. Often it makes us feel Christ has rejected us and wants nothing to do with us.

MARY'S RESPONSE

As we talked, the question foremost in Mary's mind soon became apparent. She asked me through tears and an abject sense of personal rejection: "How can God love anyone as defiled as I am?"

It's at such points I wish I could take such people and wrap them in the arms of Jesus and tell them, "He loves you just as you are and will always love you."

Unfortunately, it doesn't work as easily as all that. Yes, Jesus loved Mary and would always love her, but often accepting and assimilating that love takes time and spiritual growth. I told Mary without hesitation, "God loves you perfectly, and no stain or dirt in your life can change that." I then turned to various Scriptures about the love of God and His power to cleanse even the worst sins—none of which she'd committed—and told her that Christ died to free her from this noose of Satan.

As her heart softened in the glow of the idea that God could love one like her, I gradually turned to what I felt was the deeper issue and the one crucial to her own escape from the pit Satan had dug for her. I said, "I believe the root problem here is that you need to forgive your stepfather the same way God forgave you. I know that sounds difficult, even impossible, but God will give you the power to choose to forgive your stepfather. If you are willing, I believe it's the key to your freedom from this anger."

Mary said, "I know I am a believer in Christ and I know the Lord forgave me of all my sin when I was saved."

But could she actually forgive her stepfather?

It seemed incredible to simply by fiat forgive this man who had wreaked such havoc and damage in her life. But what else was there to do? Blow him away with a shotgun? That would only lead to worse problems. Hate him and revile him to his face? Again, it might satisfy for the moment, but in the long run it wouldn't solve the deeper problem. Just forget it? That was impossible.

Forgiveness was the only route out of this hell.

As we talked on, Mary began to visualize what the Lord was asking her to do. I watched as her face and expressions showed that a severe battle raged inside her mind. Truth and error cannot coexist, so they will fight against each other like lions in a pit. Even as I watched, I was praying that the lion of truth would win over the lion of error.

I said nothing for the next twenty minutes as Mary pounded her fists into the chair. She screamed over and over again, at me, at God, at the lies the devil was hurling into her mind at that moment. "I don't want to forgive him; he destroyed my life."

Again I wanted to show Mary that the arms of Christ beckoned, and to have her take refuge in Him. However, when the soul is doing hand-to-hand combat with the enemy, it's often best to simply listen and pray, as though the person were one's own precious child fighting for air.

The screaming and pounding went on for a long time. Gradually, her body covered with perspiration, Mary stopped and stared at me, vacant-eyed, but for the first time her face showed a glimmer of hope. I just whispered, "Give it all to Him, Mary."

As if finally gripped in the arms of the Lord Himself, Mary chose to pray: "Father in Heaven, I choose as an act of my will to forgive my stepfather of everything. . . ."

Over the next minutes she listed unspeakable abuses I could not repeat if I wanted to. Her lone voice in my office went on and on, as if Jesus Himself stood before her, reaching out and embracing her as each horrible deed was revealed. At the end, she said, "I release my stepfather to you from my heart. I turn him over to your wise justice. Father, please forgive me for my bitterness, anger, hate, and lack of forgiveness. Please take back the ground that Satan gained in my soul. I choose to live joyfully, despite the fact that there will still be results of his sin against me. I trust you. In Jesus' name, Amen."

FINDING PEACE

Tears burned in my eyes as I listened. Then tremendous relief gripped my heart. I felt that joy every Christian counselor experiences when they see someone released from the prison of anger, hatred, and Satan's steely bonds.

To my astonishment, Mary looked up and exclaimed, "I feel peace, Dr. Copley, real peace. All the rage seems to be gone."

It doesn't always happen that way. Sometimes the genuine sense of peace rises gradually, like the coming dawn after a long, dark night. But in this case, I sensed Mary's feelings were genuine. God had released her from her prison and given her the eagle's wings of true freedom in Christ.

Over the next few weeks, with her doctor's permission, Mary stopped taking her medication. Five years later she continues to grow and excel as a believer. Over our next few sessions, I encouraged Mary to read the Scriptures daily and to keep a journal of the thoughts the Lord had impressed upon her heart. I also suggested she list any special blessings that came her way along with her daily struggles. I asked her to consider becoming part of a church and getting joyfully involved.

She did all of it and is a free woman today.

It sometimes seems simplistic to some. To forgive her stepfather was all that was needed? No; actually Mary would still have moments of doubt and anger. She would still have to battle the lies that Satan tried to hurl into her mind despite her act of forgiveness and submission to Jesus. But that simple regimen of God's Word, prayer, journaling, and faithful church involvement was a key to Mary's survival and inner healing. It's often the surest prescription to health in a severe battle with the devil.

THE FIRST LIE

I believe Mary, like many who come to Christian counselors for help, had become a victim of Satan's lies. He had lied to Mary repeatedly about everything, from deserving the abuse to thinking about murdering her stepfather. She was trapped in those lies, not believing she could ever escape.

Though she had not seen her stepfather in years, she still felt influenced and overwhelmed by him. She believed he had ruined her life. Thus the first lie the enemy used on Mary was "Because of the abuse, your life is destroyed and beyond hope."

Satan knows that if he can keep us focused on our pain, we have little or no time to focus on the Lord Jesus Christ and the truth that can heal us. Mary believed that she was an inferior, worthless, and rejected person. She also believed no decent man would ever want her. That was all changed as she learned the truth—about God, His love, and His power to transform her.

A SECOND LIE

A second lie the great deceiver used on Mary was "You are unimportant, a mistake; you should never have been born."

People who feel deep rejection and worthlessness often fall prey to this lie. Mary believed she somehow deserved what happened to her. Thus, she hoped only for revenge. When the Holy Spirit brought God's truth to her heart, though, she began to understand that through Him she was not trapped. When she was a child, Satan had used the words, manipulations, and physical superiority of her stepfather. This kept her from trying to escape by going to the authorities (which were not as sensitive to these things as they are now), by telling her mother (who may not have believed her—another device of Satan), or by simply fighting back.

But now as an adult, God was able to show Mary the way out. Her life was not ruined; He had a wonderful plan for her. Rather than being inferior, she saw she was "fearfully and wonderfully made" (Psalm 139:14). Rather than seeing herself as the sick, needy one, she realized it was her stepfather, not her, who was the enslaved one. By forgiving him, she was able to release all rights of revenge to God. Truth conquered Satan's lies and she was set free.

HOW SATAN BINDS

I use Mary's case as an example of how Satan binds us and grinds our hearts into the dust. He is not content merely to stop us from witnessing or living decent Christian lives. No, his malice is so great that when he finds a truly vulnerable soul, he enjoys taking his hatred of God to the limits, and thus beating that child of God into the ground until he or she is little more than pulp.

But even then, God refuses to let Satan have his way. He steps in at various points, leading us to the truth that will set us free. I find that God always brings good out of bad. If we will trust Him, He will repair our lives, take back the lost ground, and make us live in His truth and freedom forever after. That will make whatever pain we have suffered a faint memory in the annals of time as we spend eternity in the loving presence of our Lord who does all things well.

Spiritual warfare like this happens every day in the lives of God's people. Your situation may not involve something as severe as sexual abuse. But I submit that you probably believe some lies of the great deceiver right now that keep you from experiencing the fullness of God's power and love. In this book, I will expose for you those lies and show you ways to conquer them and move on into God's great plan, taking the giant steps He intends for all His children.

CHAPTER TWO

THE TRUTH
ABOUT
SPIRITUAL
WARFARE

Is spiritual warfare a common occurrence for Christians? Or is spiritual warfare a scare tactic to get Christians in line?

"God would never let Christians be tested by the devil." "'Spiritual warfare' is a phony phrase. We already have spiritual victory." "Spiritual warfare is a concept that only kooks believe." I've heard these responses and more to the statement Christians are in a spiritual battle. But such beliefs are right out of the pit. Furthermore, they contradict the Scriptures.

It's true that we are born again by the Spirit of God. We begin a vibrant new life (2 Corinthians 5:17). But we also are joined in a battle—a battle from which dying and arriving in heaven will be our only escape. This battle is called *spiritual warfare*. Such warfare appears on nearly every page of Scripture, from the beginning when Adam and Eve fell to the lies of Satan, through the journeys of Israel as they listened to more lies of the devil. It led finally to the coming of Jesus and the arena of entrenched falsehood that He entered, which ultimately led to His death.

THE FINAL OUTCOME: VICTORY

Through it all, though, a reassuring theme runs through the Bible: God is ultimately in control; nothing happens outside His sovereignty, and even Satan is little more than a player in God's vast drama. God has every lie and machination well in hand. The Scriptures declare that nothing Satan does will deter the triumph of God's plan, which is the establishment of the kingdom that will last forever.

The New Testament describes the battle as continuous and purposeful. In Ephesians 6:10–18, the classic passage detailing the spiritual armor that every Christian must carry into battle, the apostle Paul gave this call to arms:

Put on the whole armor of God, that you may be able to stand against the wiles of the devil. For we do not wrestle against flesh and blood, but against principalities, against powers, against the rulers of the darkness of this age, against spiritual hosts of wickedness in the heavenly places. Therefore take up the whole armor of God, that you may be able to withstand in the evil day, and having done all, to stand. (Verses 11–13)

And the apostle Peter cautioned all believers about the leader of the attacks: "Be vigilant; because your adversary the devil walks about like a roaring lion" (1 Peter 5:8).

Satan is in a fierce battle with God and His followers, but his fate is sealed, for God has already won the victory. As Christians, we fight *from* victory, not *for* victory. Such victory is not always a reality in our Christian lives, however. Paul exhorted Timothy to "wage the good warfare" (1 Timothy 1:18). But truthfully, most Christians know very little about the enemy or the warfare he wages against us and which we must wage against him. As a result, we do not walk in the spiritual victory that is ours in Christ Jesus.

TEMPORARY ADVANCES
BY THE GREAT DECEIVER

Years ago, I heard a man speak on spiritual warfare in a way that raised the hair on the back of my neck. The casting out of demons, frontal attacks on Satan through rebuking prayer, and loud denunciations of the enemy using biblical language, all crackled through his speech. Today, I honestly question that speaker's accuracy in describing real spiritual warfare. True, there are moments when the casting out of a demon is necessary. And yes, prayer is essential in defeating the power of Satan in a believer's life. But warfare does not involve attacking Satan himself. Instead, spiritual warfare means confronting the enemy's lies with God's truth, as I showed in the previous chapter.

In warfare counseling, I have found people face mainly two problems: they sin and they believe lies. Satan's only real power is through those lies. He will take God's truth and twist it or deny it. In tempting Eve, for instance, the serpent (inhabited by Satan) twisted God's words (Genesis 3:1) and directly denied them (verse 4).

Satan succeeds as the great deceiver when we believe in our mind and emotions what he says is true even though it is false. Liberty comes when we grasp and believe the truth. At that point we are no longer deceived. Satan's advances against us are foiled.

Why is this deception so sinister? Because we live what we believe. When I believe a lie, I live that lie. If I think I'm worthless, I am worthless. If I come to believe hatred is justified, then I will feel just in hating. Satan foments anger and all sorts of negative emotions with such lies.

This is why warfare is so much more a matter of the heart and mind than of exorcism and so many other dramatic examples others give to the issue. I believe that in America today more people are susceptible to the subtle lies of Satan than any kind of oppression or possession through the occult. Though the occult is gaining a much greater foothold, even to those trapped in its bonds, it's not actual indwelling of spirits that occurs, but a series of lies being accepted and followed as the truth that destroys them.

THE LIES WE HEAR AND ACCEPT

You need not be in the occult to hear and accept Satan's lies. Many Christians are listening to his lies. Some are as simple yet devastating as someone telling himself that he's stupid.

I believed this lie for many years. I thought I was an idiot, a person with a low IQ who would never amount to much more in life than working in the most menial jobs. I just thought I didn't have the brains for a "real" job.

This belief went back to second and third grades, when an abusive teacher called me stupid nearly every day and often hit me with a ruler. Eventually, I decided never to study or try to please any teacher again. I believed in my heart that teachers were the enemy. I also thought I was just too dumb to learn from them. Years later I graduated from high school with a D minus average. I wasn't proud of it, but I believed it was just deserts: I was stupid; I got what I deserved.

But then something happened: I accepted Christ at age twenty-one. Shortly thereafter, the Lord called me to attend college to prepare to do His work. I remember telling the Lord, "I'm too stupid to go to college."

THE POWER OF BIBLICAL TRUTH

God then spoke to my heart, saying, "I will go with you. I will help you."

That, of course, is truth. It's based on the Scriptures (Hebrews 13:5, for example).

Hearing those words in my heart was an astonishing moment of hope charged with faith, something I'd rarely experienced. I decided to take God up on it, even though I did have some serious doubts about my abilities as a college student.

Somehow I made it through college and then discovered God wanted me to attend seminary. Again, I was amazed He might want someone as stupid as me in His work. In fact, I couldn't find anyone in the Bible I considered as dumb as me, so in many ways none of this made sense. Why did He want me? The feeling of being stupid dogged me every step of the way, and I remember in seminary feeling awful. "I'm such a dope," I told myself.

One day, though, always looking for some proof that I was wrong, I happened upon Psalm 139:14: "I am fearfully and wonderfully made."

It was one of those moments when the Spirit of God simply grasps your soul and won't let go. I sat there stunned as the Holy Spirit spoke to my heart and said, "I have given you adequate intelligence. You will have the ability, through me, to do what you are called to do."

I didn't have an IQ of 165. I didn't have the brains to find a cure for cancer. I certainly lacked the preaching ability of a Billy Graham. But for me, those words were incredible: "I am fearfully and wonderfully made." I wasn't stupid.

For a moment I sat there in awe of God's words to me; and then I simply thought, "OK, if He says so, I'll accept it." With real vigor, peace flooded my heart. I can never forget it, because from that day on, the problem of my intellect was solved. Satan's lie that I was stupid was gone.

Can it really be that simple? Often it is. God's truth can destroy a lie like Sammy Sosa destroying a baseball on an 0–2 count!

The amazing thing is that many people will go through life believing such a lie and never recover or learn the truth. How does Satan manage it? Because he whispers the lie so subtly and so repeatedly that we cannot think any other way.

SOME COMMON OBJECTIONS
TO SPIRITUAL WARFARE

Some Christians do not fall for these lies, of course. But many buy the lie that spiritual warfare proponents are fanatics, or kooks, or worse. They accept this because of three extreme responses they have observed. Let's take a moment to deal with each of these responses.

The first objection I find occurs among Christians who witness other believers who fear demons are involved in every little problem. Such believers create what I call "the demon under every bush" problem. Groups that see Satan as this active and involved in Christians' lives are quick to rush in and cast out various spirits, going so far as to exorcise a "spirit of overeating," or a "spirit of anger," or a "spirit of swearing." This is absurd, you might say, but there are groups that see warfare in these terms. Exorcisms like this are usually unnecessary and in fact the very thing Satan wants us in some cases to do—to see him as so present and overwhelming that every other word must be a "casting out," or a "prayer against the devil." Such actions look weird and few people understand what such folks are all about.

A second objection comes from Christians seeing the even greater extreme of people who go about brushing "demons" off their grocery sacks before entering their home. This is not only ludicrous, but it focuses on the devil in a very unhealthy way. Believers in such bondage to rituals can act and think like people with obsessive-compulsive disorder (OCD), who can't go anywhere without washing their hands sixteen times. This is just another lie Satan uses to keep us from the truth.

A third objection is raised: They see believers who try to get demons to actually speak out of a person. Supposedly, through hearing a demon speak, proponents of this approach believe they will learn deep and dark things about their kingdom as well as God's. Of course, this teaching is at once extreme and sensational. And Satan uses it to convince some to think, *See, this is just a bunch of fear tactics and high drama.* Some leaders persist in teaching this, even though God's Word tells us not to listen to the "doctrines of demons" (see 1 Timothy 4:1).

All these objections point out clear excesses that in themselves are lies of the devil. They get people focused on the wrong things, a favorite tactic of Satan. He loves to divert counselors and others from the real issues.

THE WORLD, FLESH, AND DEVIL WORK TOGETHER

It's also true that all temptation isn't from spiritual warfare. The world, the flesh, and the demonic world all work together in temptation. The flesh is like a beast in the basement, which will raise its head at times and exert its influence. We are sinners by nature. We have a natural "bent" to choose to sin. While we might claim Satan gave us the suggestion, there comes a point at which Satan doesn't even need to suggest the sin anymore—we just walk off into it because we like it, even crave it. That's the flesh speaking.

The world, too, exerts an influence. Its lies, suggestions, tricks, and pressures all can lead us into sin as effectively as anything the devil might throw at us. As in the parable of the sower, the world sends weeds and thistles that choke out the truth in a believer's life until he is all but ruined. Satan uses the world to promote his lies of wealth without conscience, pleasure without consequences, and long life without worry about judgment.

The fact that not all temptation comes from the spiritual conflict with Satan and his legions does not mean that spiritual conflict is myth. Instead, Satan uses the temptation of the flesh and the world for his evil purpose. He also uses false doctrine to make Christians vulnerable to his deceptions. Jesus spoke about this in Matthew 13, in His parable of the wheat and the tares. Satan sowed tares among the wheat. Strangely enough, tares look exactly like wheat until the very end of the harvest, when the wheat develops its "head of kernels," something the tares never have. Jesus made the point that Satan sends his tares—pretend believers—into the church. They look like the real thing and will continue to look like that until the end. Meanwhile, they will plant their sinister suggestions and diversions that keep a church from the important tasks of evangelism of the lost and edification of believers.

It's through marshalling all these forces that Satan attacks best. But if you don't believe Satan is out and about, why worry about him? "Enjoy your life," some say. "There's nothing to fear." Nonetheless, a thief is never so dangerous as when people believe he has left town. The enemy of our soul loves to have us think he is no longer around.

I believe Satan nurtures lies everywhere he can. It's one more reason a warfare outlook is so essential to defeating the devil when he attacks.

Why is rejecting the reality of Satan so foolish? Because it leads people in power to make decisions without considering his activity or presence. It leads counselors to try to solve problems without attacking the real problem. And it leads pastors to preach a powerless gospel that frees no one from the enemy—because there is no enemy!

Again, my own experience proves this problem. I attended four years of Bible college and six years of graduate school. During this time, godly professors diligently instructed me to teach God's truth. In the process, though, I was taught very little about spiritual warfare. Their apparent fear was that focusing on the enemy would bring anxiety and paranoia into the church. I remember one professor who railed about how one church he knew became "so demon-conscious they lost their focus on God."

SATAN IS ACTIVE:
THE TESTIMONY OF MISSIONS

The truth of Satan's active warfare is not fully ignored in Christian schools. In many evangelical schools, missions professors teach the reality of spiritual warfare. These professors usually have been on mission fields where they have encountered warfare face-to-face. When I visited eastern Africa on an assignment, I didn't have to tell my students that spiritual warfare was real. They saw firsthand the power of the witch doctor. In witnessing pagan worship, the students and I saw and heard demons manifest themselves and speak through overpowered victims. Some Africans testified of being demonized before they came to Christ. Others told me about the power of curses and spells and how their unsaved family members desperately feared the demonic world.

When you see things like this in person, you can't help but accept the reality of spiritual warfare.

Once I was confronted with my own failure to emphasize the spiritual battle when a former seminary student of mine named Sam traveled to the Philippines as a missionary. At the end of his first term, he returned home and had lunch with me. His first question was "Why didn't you teach me about the reality of the enemy?" When I asked what he meant, Sam said, "I faced spiritual attacks that I was not aware of. I was never told warfare was even possible. I would have been easily defeated had I not attended a seminar by a warfare leader who came to the Philippines. His teachings enabled me to recognize what was happening in my ministry."

I asked Sam's forgiveness and explained that as his professor I was ignorant of the lies and tactics of the enemy at the time.

A PERSONAL CONFRONTATION
WITH THE ENEMY

I then explained to Sam how I came to a painful understanding of Satan's work in the world. As a conservative pastor, I had preached against those who held a warfare position, thinking I was exposing error.

I recalled how I accidentally received a tape by Dr. Jim Logan on spiritual warfare. We had ordered a series of tapes from a Christian ministry and somehow they included one of Jim's messages. One evening after reading the Bible to my family, I asked my wife to play the tape. Ten minutes into it I asked her to shut off the tape and put it in the garbage. I then told my children that Dr. Logan was teaching heresy. The next Sunday I renounced him and his ministry from the pulpit, requesting that if anyone present owned any of his tapes or materials to burn them.

This foolish viewpoint soon received a karate chop that would cut me to the heart. Two months later, our oldest son shared with my wife, Elizabeth, and me that he had a spirit guide who was with him in a supernatural way. He talked with him all the time. After hearing him out, I said to Elizabeth, "Let's ignore it. Maybe it will go away."

It didn't. Things quickly spun out of control and took turns so weird and bad that Elizabeth finally asked if she could talk to Jim Logan about it. I said, "Five minutes; don't give him our name." In the conversation she gave enough details about me that Jim was able to get my phone number from a mutual friend.

One morning he called and said, "Good morning, Ken! This is Jim Logan."

Being a bit brash and put off, I said, "Let me tell you what I did with your tape and what I said to the congregation that I pastor."

Jim laughed after I explained and said, "God has a tremendous sense of humor."

With that bit of wit, the ice melted and I confessed, "I am desperate and I don't have a clue as to how to help my son."

Jim questioned me for thirty minutes, then said, "I believe the Lord wants me to lead you through a doctoral-level course in spiritual warfare. It's obvious you haven't been to kindergarten where warfare is concerned."

Jim kept his word; he helped me understand the nature of the warfare around me and guided me in helping my son. My son was set free, and now I have at least graduated from kindergarten. (Dr. Logan continues to have a successful ministry in spiritual warfare counseling and has written an effective book on spiritual warfare, *Reclaiming Surrendered Ground*.)

If you're one of those readers who scorns the whole idea of spiritual warfare, let me say up front that I used to be a kindred spirit. But reality has a way of smashing your arguments into dust. My view of the world changed as I saw the reality of the enemy and the reality of Christ's power. The contrast between the purposes of the two became obvious as I considered Christ's words: "The thief does not come except to steal, and to kill, and to destroy. I have come that they may have life, and that they may have it more abundantly" (John 10:10).

BEAUTIFUL IN GOD'S EYES

Let me give you an example of a person who, through changing her worldview, was set free from the power of the devil and given the joy of serving God in freedom and power.

She was an extremely attractive young woman I'll call Jill, who came into my office weeping. After ten minutes of her sobbing and me trying to comfort her and find out what was wrong, Jill confessed she believed she was ugly. The very notion made me want to laugh. Her, ugly? If she was ugly, I must have been a hyena. And yet, it's such a common feeling, especially among women in today's world. Everyone wants to be Barbie or Cindy Crawford.

This was a variation on the lie I believed about being stupid, but it's a common deception of Satan.

As she wept, I said to Jill, trying to move her in the direction of the truth, "Are you willing to accept yourself as God—loving, wise, compassionate, all-knowing God—made you, or do you think He made a mistake?"

As a Christian, she didn't believe God made mistakes, but this was a completely new concept to her.

When she stammered out "no" to my query about accepting herself, I read the passage in Psalms 139:14, reminding her about being "fearfully and wonderfully made." I explained God had made each of us beautiful and amazing creations in our own right, a perfect creature of His love and wisdom. While yes, the world might look on and criticize, the truth was God had made Jill exactly as He'd wanted, and what He'd wanted was to fashion her "fearfully"—someone to respect and reverence—and "wonderfully"—someone amazing and perfect and beautiful in the eyes of Perfect Love and Wisdom.

As we talked, the Holy Spirit opened her heart. For the first time, she saw that a good, wise, and loving God had created her as He had wanted to all along. She realized He had given her traits, abilities, and even physical characteristics that He considered beautiful and immeasurably attractive.

As I shared these things, an astonishing transformation came over her face, a radiance that proved she had accepted herself in a healing, freedom-giving way because of God's truth.

Months later she told me that she could not only enjoy the way she looked, but she saw that all of herself—her mind, her personality, her heart and soul—was "fearfully and wonderfully made" by the God who knows all! This was not arrogance, nor even conceit. The fact was she no longer compared her looks to others or to billboards. God had set her free.

At a later time she told me, "I have peace about how I look because I know the Lord made me exactly the way He wanted."

Had Jill been under spiritual attack? Had Satan engaged her in spiritual warfare? Definitely. Jill had believed lies hammered into her by the devil through the world and the flesh and probably other sources as well. Those lies had debilitated her, made her doubt herself at every turn, and even made her hate herself. What could this be but Satan's plan to destroy the good thing God created?

WHAT ABOUT YOU?

If you've read this chapter and still believe spiritual warfare is a type of baloney, I implore you: Recognize the spiritual battle around you.

Realize Satan has power on earth (Luke 22:53; Ephesians 6:12). But also realize God has greater power (1 John 4:4). You need not fear (that is, hold in awe) Satan. No, the one to truly fear in a reverential sense is God. He loves you and will guide you through any warfare you will face today, this week, and all the way to the end of your life. Rejoice that He is with you every step of the path. Take this warfare seriously, but at the same time keep your heart set on the things above where Christ is at the right hand of God. That will still your soul when you hear that lion roar.

CHAPTER THREE

WHO IS SATAN AND HOW DOES HE WORK?

You may be surprised that Satan has personality, great power, and a sinister plan. You may have viewed him as some cartoon character with horns and a long tail, dressed in a red suit. That's another lie. Well, then, who is this devil who wreaks such havoc in our lives?

His original name was Lucifer, son of the morning (Isaiah 14:12), God's masterpiece (Ezekiel 28:12), and a guardian cherub (Ezekiel 28:14). He "walked . . . in the midst of fiery stones" (verse 14) and functioned as God's highest creation, perhaps leader over all the created angels. God employed Lucifer in revealing the great truths about Himself and counted on Lucifer to teach the angelic hordes about God, His person, personality, works, and plans.

So originally the devil was a good angel, gifted by God and loyal in his actions. What happened?

LUCIFER'S REBELLION

Lucifer envied God. He envied the worship God received, the adulation of the billions in heaven. He began to lust after what God possessed. He wanted to be like God, to take God's place (Isaiah 14:13–14). This led him to rebel and incite an attack on God unlike any war in human history. Some think World War II was bad. Yes, that war had an impact on the world. But in its scope and ultimate importance, this rebellion made WWII look like a wrestling match in kindergarten.

Undoubtedly, God warned Lucifer, but ultimately God had to let Lucifer make his own choices. He would not force Lucifer to worship or even serve Him. Lucifer had the right to refuse, and he exercised it.

When God warned him, Lucifer refused to repent and he persuaded a third of the angels of heaven to follow him in his rebellion. Perhaps he promised them places of power and some kind of weird notion of "creative freedom." Whatever it was, they followed and sank with Lucifer's ship. God defeated him summarily.

God then created Adam and Eve, set them in a perfect environment, and subjected them to one test, giving them the right to choose—to choose either to obey or ignore God. The test was whether they would eat of a certain tree's fruit that God had commanded them to avoid.

At that point, Lucifer, now Satan, stepped in and tempted the first human couple. By leading our first parents into sin, he immediately defiled God's perfect creation. That plunged the whole universe into a condition of spiritual death that only the death and resurrection of Christ could repair.

Today, Satan roams our planet looking for people he can enslave to himself. He uses lies to accomplish that end. His plan is to deceive us into thinking such thoughts as "Jesus was just a good man; His life and death mean no more than any other person's," and "No one needs some special act of faith in Jesus to find redemption."

If Satan fails in that mission and people come to a personal relationship with Christ through faith, Satan tells those new believers another lie: "Spiritual growth, personal development, and learning God's

Word are not important for spiritual maturity." The great deceiver says to believers, "Forget the church, because it's full of hypocrites. Find your own way in this world." And he teaches the world's philosophy of success: "Remember, health, wealth, and power are the primary elements of true success."

WHO IS THIS ENEMY?

If you want to understand Satan's sinister plan, a good place to start is Isaiah 14:12–14. Here you will find several important facts about the enemy. First, when Satan attacked God, he made five gargantuan, prideful statements of his objectives. His five "I Wills" are revealing. They are:

- "I will ascend into heaven."
- "I will exalt my throne above the stars of God."
- "I will sit on the mount of the congregation on the farthest sides of the north."
- "I will ascend above the heights of the clouds."
- "I will be like the Most High."

Behind those boasts is his sinister plan. We can describe it this way. Satan then and now wants:

1. To ascend to God's realm and take charge.
2. To rule over all creation in God's place.
3. To lead in all worship services that were meant to worship God.
4. To break into God's most private secret haven.
5. To drive God out and take His place.

Satan was vowing to assassinate God, to take His place and rule everything—no more; no less.

At rock bottom, this is the ultimate expression of pride. "I will be number one, on my own, answering to no one!"

SATAN'S FIRST ATTACK ON PEOPLE

God dealt with this upstart rather quickly and cast him out of heaven, defeating him with a mere word. All Satan's boasts crumpled to nothing, and he found himself somewhere in a whole new, God-created universe. Satan had blood on his mind, and he soon discovered this world called earth, populated by all sorts of amazing creatures, most notably two who were in many ways like the angels of heaven. God called them Adam and Eve, and He gave them total freedom minus one: They could not eat of a certain tree. If they did, dire consequences would follow.

Wasting no time at all, Satan thought up Plan B and decided if he couldn't defeat God, he'd mess up God's handiwork so badly that God would have to admit failure and give up. That was and is Satan's sinister plan. He desires to defeat God and God's good plan. His first step would be to get these perfect folks out of the clutches of God. So Satan visited the Garden of Eden disguised as a serpent.

This is one of his bedrock principles of deception: Never come as you are; always use a pleasant disguise. The serpent was the most "cunning" of all God's animals, according to Genesis 3:1. This means not only was he smart, but he was beautiful, friendly, and charming.

Once he had possessed the serpent, Satan got to the point quickly. God had commanded Adam (probably not directly to Eve) that he couldn't eat from the Tree of the Knowledge of Good and Evil, because if he did, he would die. This was a test designed by God to prove whether Adam and Eve would be loyal to Him and obey Him in a simple matter. All real obedience proceeds by us obeying God about seemingly trivial things.

As the serpent, Satan asked Eve, "Has God indeed said, 'You shall not eat of every tree of the garden?'"

Satan's motive here was to get Eve to think the fruit was not only forbidden but that God was holding back something good. This would cast doubt on God's love for Eve. If God really loved her, He would not have kept from her any good thing.

It's not surprising that Satan tells us the same lie today. "Why wait to have sex until marriage? God just wants to keep something good from you. There's no harm in it." And, "Go ahead and try those drugs. They won't hurt you. God knows they will make you more creative and even more intelligent, to say nothing of happier. In fact, that's why He doesn't want you to try them!"

Satan always arouses discontent with what God wants and then assures us God is withholding it from us because He knows how happy it will make us. Or rich. Or powerful.

Answering Satan, Eve said, "We may eat the fruit of the trees of the garden; but of the fruit of the tree which is in the midst of the garden, God has said, 'You shall not eat it, nor shall you touch it, lest you die'" (Genesis 3:2–3).

Notice: God never said, "nor shall you touch it" (see His words in Genesis 2:17). Eve was already demonstrating an attitude of discontent toward God. The enemy found the spark he could fan into a flame. When we are discontent, we tend to distort God's Word. And Eve was ready to hear Satan's distorted rendering of God's command.

At that point, Satan knew he could lie directly. He said, "You will not surely die. For God knows that in the day you eat of it your eyes will be opened, and you will be like God, knowing good and evil" (verses 4–5). In essence, Satan was saying, "You will be the one who knows, decides, and determines good and evil. You'll be in control. If you eat of the tree, you'll be your own god; you'll call the shots—you will be the boss. You won't have God telling you what to do anymore!"

Satan works through the flesh to tempt us to be dissatisfied with God and all He gives us. We are then more willing to grab and eat the "forbidden fruit." Only later do we realize the "apple" has worms in it. Satan persuaded Eve to eat the fruit and Eve then went to Adam, who also capitulated.

Moments later, the Bible says, "Adam and his wife hid themselves from the presence of the Lord God" (Genesis 3:8). Sin always causes fear. We believe God will punish us severely for our mistake and that He will never show love to us again, which is one more lie of the enemy.

The truth came out, though, as God went looking for Adam. "Then the Lord God called to Adam and said to him, 'Where are you?'" (verse 9). The Lord hadn't rejected Adam or Eve even though He knew what they had done. He still loved Adam despite his sin.

BACK TO THE PRESENT WORLD

Several years ago, I worked at a youth center in Indianapolis. While on staff there, I counseled with juvenile delinquents from the inner city and youth with felony convictions from around the country. While talking with these young people, I would often ask, "Do you feel that you are in charge of your life?" A typical answer was "Absolutely. I'm the one in control of my life. No one tells me what to do."

Next I would ask, "Did you come up with that idea on your own, or did someone come up with that idea before you did?"

I wasn't trying to put them down, just to show them this wasn't an original idea on their part; it was a lie foisted on us from long ago. Usually, when I asked that question, they couldn't come up with an answer. At that point, I'd turn first to Isaiah 14 and then Genesis 3 and say, "Satan actually came up with that idea first." I would show them how Satan originated the "I am in charge" idea millennia ago. He then sold it to Eve and Adam. They ate the fruit that caused spiritual and ultimately physical death. Had they not believed that God would send a Savior into the world to crush and defeat Satan in a final sense, they would have died eternally as well.

At this point, some of these teens would exclaim, "I have been acting just like Satan."

This opened a crack in the door that let God's light shine into their hearts. As I showed them more biblical truth, many became receptive to the gospel of Jesus Christ.

Ultimately, these two passages, Isaiah 14 and Genesis 3, show the most basic of Satan's strategy, declared in two big lies. First lie: You can and will take charge of your life, and God is not necessary. Second lie: God is holding you back; throw off His shackles and you'll be truly free to do as you want.

These lies stand at the root of almost all sin problems. For instance, "Drugs are a way to be happy, and you can get them readily. God's way, which is holiness, is boring, painful, and makes you feel lousy all the time." Or consider the temptation of adultery. "An affair will get you what you want now." And even every form of abuse of another person is just another way of saying, "I will take from you what I want because I own you."

This is the essence of spiritual warfare—Satan using lies to get us to sin against God and then keep on sinning as if there is no God.

What then are the primary lies of Satan? We'll look at that in the next chapter.

CHAPTER FOUR

THE PRIMARY DECEPTIONS OF SATAN AND HIS COHORTS

When Alice visited my office, it quickly became clear she felt desperate. After all, her psychologist had given her up as being hopeless. She opened our first session with these challenging words: "I probably know as much about biblical counseling as you do. I have read every book I know on the subject."

After six more sessions, I concluded she was right. In her mind she knew the truth, but in the depth of her being, she believed a whole cacophony of lies that left her feeling guilty and tainted—thus her sense of desperation.

Her mind seemed bombarded with horrid, even evil thoughts: "You're worthless"; "Nobody wants you"; "Kill your mother, brother, yourself." Along with the thoughts came terrible feelings of hopelessness and impotence.

In a few minutes I discovered that despite these horrible inner feelings, Alice was an intelligent, personable, and beautiful young woman. A junior in college, she made excellent grades. But her spiritual and emotional life left her totally defeated. During one session, a breakthrough idea occurred to me. Jim was her prayer partner for the week. I motioned to him, seated at the back of the room, and said to Alice in my most authoritative voice, "I command you to get up, go to the back of the room, and punch Jim in the mouth with all of your might."

Alice glared at me and said, "I won't do that!"

"Do what?" I asked.

"I won't punch Jim in the mouth."

"Have you been thinking about punching Jim in the mouth?" I answered. "Where did that come from?

"What an awful, horrible person you must be to think such a thing!" I continued. "In fact, I think I'll leave. I certainly shouldn't stay in the same room with a person like you and I'm going to leave now!"

As I moved toward the door, she yelled at me. "Just a minute! You put the thought in my mind, and now you are accusing me of thinking it! I didn't think that up. You said it to me!"

Instantly, like the lights snapping on in a darkened room, it dawned on her that that was precisely what Satan had done with her—planted twisted thoughts and made her think they were her own genuine motivations and desires.

Recently Alice called to tell me she was doing well. I asked her how I'd helped her and she related that my illustration of the enemy's intruding thoughts enabled her to see the truth about the enemy's ability to plant thoughts in our minds and make us think they're our own. For years she had heard of such a thing, but in that counseling session God moved it from her head to her heart.

How then does the enemy work? He operates through strategies based on lies about God and about us. Follow through these common methods.

STRATEGY ONE: Thoughts in Our Minds

Planting twisted, evil thoughts in our minds is Satan's primary tactic in leading us into sin. I have often wondered how many killers, rapists, child molesters, and abusers were led into their destructive ways through thoughts planted by the enemy. The power of suggestion is an awesome thing, as any hypnotist can attest. Satan will plant a thought, nurture it, deal with our arguments, and try to persuade us to take sinful action. When we do and get a "charge" out of it, as all sin provides initially, he sits back and lets us run with it. Soon, he's out of a job and we're sinning along like there's no tomorrow.

But Satan isn't the only one who can lead or motivate us through thought-plants. God can, too. However, His thoughts are altogether good and right.

A good example of a thought planted by God can be found in Matthew 16:13–17, where Simon Peter answered Jesus' question, "Who do men say that I, the Son of Man, am?" He said, "You are the Christ, the Son of the living God." Where did this realization come from? Peter didn't dream it up on his own. No, Jesus follows Peter's answer with the statement that God Himself revealed it to him.

Clearly, both God and Satan are in the thought-planting business. Remember, though, God only sows good, wholesome, truthful thoughts. He would never tell anyone to commit sin, even though criminals have claimed at times that God "told them to do" their crime.

In a swift turnaround, Satan attacked Peter in the next few seconds after Peter's declaration that Jesus was the Messiah. Perhaps Satan attacked in retribution, perhaps because he saw an opportunity in the pride that Peter may have felt because of his swift and correct answer about Jesus' identity. When Jesus told His disciples He would die in Jerusalem, Peter protested, saying, "This shall not happen to You!" Jesus immediately rebuked him, saying, "Get behind Me, Satan!"

Jesus had quickly recognized the source of Peter's words. Clearly, this thought was not from God or even Peter, but from the devil.

In such circumstances, we see the essence of the spiritual battle. God can plant a thought: "Why don't you read your Bible now?" And Satan can immediately counter it: "Hey, aren't you hungry? Better see what's in the fridge first!" Suddenly, a battle rages in your heart: read the Bible or eat food? The choice is yours, but the suggestions may have come from the spiritual realm.

Any and all of it can be directly out of the mouth of the forces of darkness.

Let's be clear here about something important: It is not sin for us to have wrong thoughts. Merely "hearing" a thought flit through your brain inciting you to the most diabolical evil is not in itself sin. It becomes sin when we pick up on that thought, dwell on it, and then act on it (see James 1:13–15).

STRATEGY TWO: Distorting Our Belief System

A second method of attack from Satan is the distortion of our belief system. Satan distorts our belief system as he distorts who God is and who we are. The great deceiver may tempt us to believe, "Since God hates me, I ought to hate myself." Or "Since my body or parts of my body are evil, I will use them for whatever pleasure I can find." At times the enemy will say, "You can make it on your own. You don't need God; besides, He is not interested in helping you anyway." The Evil One implanted the thought and we bought into it. That is what Ananias did in Acts 5:2–3.

We reason and make decisions using both our minds and our hearts. Proverbs 23:7a says, "For as he thinks in his heart, so is he." We live what we truly believe. How we act does not always reflect what we say, but it does reflect our belief system. If your life is immoral, dishonest, proud, or depraved, it is a sure sign that your belief system is immoral, dishonest, proud, or depraved.

Linda had believed the enemy's lies since childhood. When she first came to me, she told me she was despondent, depressed, and suicidal. She had been used and abused much of her life. As a result of the immoral actions of abusive parents, her beliefs about God had become distorted. Their depraved actions and her own self-indulgence convinced Linda that God had no interest in her. "I have done so many terrible things in my life," she said, "I can't even forgive myself, let alone believe that God would forgive me!" She was broken and literally hated herself.

Probing deeper, she told me, "I can recall, even as a little child, feeling as though everyone would be better off without me. Over the years, I planned many times to kill myself." Voices taunted her, goading her into self-hatred, deeper depression, and even suicide.

We talked at length about the nature of the spirit world, how Satan influenced her and told her lies and how various strongholds had been built into her thinking. Gradually, through the use of Scripture and systematically taking each lie and exposing it, Linda began to see that her depression was largely the result of the skewed thinking Satan had nurtured in her life. She confronted each wrong thought, rejected it, and replaced it with the kinds of truths I'll show you in this book. She refused to listen to the "voices" that begged a hearing.

Some time later, she wrote me, "Today, I can honestly say I have not been depressed at all since that time spent in counseling with you, Dr. Copley. Different things in my life have saddened me, but I have not been depressed or suicidal since then! Also I have not heard voices in my mind."

Her message to people ensnared in the same kinds of depression as she is that "all is not lost. There is help out there from that Someone mightier than we are, who will come to our aid if we will just ask Him!"

Linda found that she did not have to remain a victim; she could counterattack using the Word of God to expose the enemy's lies and replace them with God's truth.

STRATEGY THREE: Sidetracking

A third device of Satan is what I call "sidetracking." I honestly think the church is the only outfit on earth that goes out to war not knowing who her enemy is. We think the enemy is the lost, or the Muslims, or the pope, or some such group of people. In reality, Satan is the true enemy, but we fight each other instead. The great deceiver succeeds with this lie, sidetracking us into fighting secondary issues rather than the main, important ones. Sidetracking occurs when Satan diverts us from the important tasks of learning to discern wolves and their ideas, and leads us into foolish pursuits—spending all our time on the pleasures of this world, the pursuit of power and wealth, or other worthless diversions that Scripture clearly condemns.

The Evil One informs us we don't need to memorize Scripture, read the Bible, or learn doctrine in detail. He "sidetracks" us into thinking that the fall social, the church bake sale, and keeping up with all the local gossip are what really matter. Or worse, he suggests that because we hear the Bible exposited verse by verse on Sunday morning that we're somehow superior to the church down the street whose pastor is more concerned about the environment, or the poor, or influencing the government. When we hear the Word but fail to put it into practice, Satan has successfully diverted us into pride, one of his best spirit-killers.

I honestly see such things as the greatest folly in the church today. Perhaps 90 percent of the men I counsel don't even read the Bible on a daily basis. Most of them haven't learned a Bible verse since they attended Sunday school as children. They all give the same excuse: "I don't have time." That is simply a lie. Satan has sidetracked them and they've bought into it. They have time to watch television, play sports, and a multitude of other things, but real discipleship and growth don't seem like such priorities. Such "sidetracks" are the methods Satan uses to keep us in chains.

How do you spot such a sidetrack and get back to the main line? Perhaps an example will help.

A chief executive officer of a large business came to me with many personal problems. I asked him if he read the Bible. He gave me the classic answer: "I don't have time." I asked him if he took breaks at work. He answered, "Of course." I then challenged him to take his Bible to work and read one proverb per day.

He did so and, in time, began reading the Scriptures thirty minutes per day. Then, after the evening meal at home, he would share with his family what God had taught him that day.

A remarkable transformation occurred over a matter of months. Today he functions as an active church member and walks closely with Christ.

When you look at your life, compare the Bible's prescribed priorities with what you are actually doing with your time. This will show if and how well Satan has sidetracked you. Perhaps you see that basic spiritual disciplines such as prayer, Bible study and memorization, church attendance and service, and sharing your faith have all been successfully pushed out of the picture. You have little motivation to show love to your family, neighbors, and strangers, though the Scriptures urge you to do so. In the place of these good disciplines are endless hours at work, hours in front of the television, and more hours spent in hobbies or "neutral" pursuits. If this is the case, you need to reconsider what you're doing.

Has Satan successfully sidetracked you into work, play, special projects, or extra sleep? None of these things is necessarily bad in itself. But that's the essence of the warfare: Satan makes you justify one or more of these activities as very important to make money or help you relax or just to give your mind a rest. Eventually they can completely stifle all spiritual involvement.

STRATEGY FOUR: Lies About God

A fourth arena Satan uses to fell us is to fill us with lies about God: "God couldn't love one like you!"; "God really can't help in this situation"; "God is far more concerned about the poor than your financial straits"; "Surely you're not going to trouble God with that trivia!" Such ideas all function as lies that not only keep us from trusting God in the crises of life, but even from seeking Him.

Lies about God are Satan's favorite deception. And, of course, such lies often distort our belief system (which is Satan's strategy number two).

Jennifer came to me perplexed. She had recently been delivered from twenty years in the occult. Despite her deliverance to Jesus, though, she believed Satan possessed more power than God. She had observed considerable demonic power as an occult participant, and had seen God seemingly powerless over such things. We prayed and searched the Scriptures, and the Holy Spirit opened her spiritual eyes to see that Satan slanders and opposes God, saying things like, "He is weak," "He can't help," "He doesn't care about your situation," and "He's busy with other things." Such lies can lead an otherwise committed believer to think, "What's the use?"

After several counseling sessions, Jennifer wrote me this letter:

Dear Dr. Copley,
I can't begin to find words to express my gratitude and praise for all the time you spent with me. The outcome is truly miraculous! I am now a free woman able to experience all the love and joy and miracles of God's bountiful blessings. I have come to know that obedience to

His Word is the key to a personal and living relationship with our loving Lord. . . .

God's truth can always overcome Satan's lies. But when we're weak in spirit and our circumstances severe, it's easier to accept the idea that God doesn't care, can't help, isn't sovereign, or doesn't really have a plan to give us hope and heart.

STRATEGY FIVE: Lies About Ourselves

Satan tells us lies about ourselves. After his rebellion, he became the father of lies (John 8:44). From his own "I wills" in Isaiah 14 to his attacks on Adam and Eve and later on Jesus, he employs one lie as his favorite: "You can be your own boss; you can be in charge of your own life." That is Satan's main way to keep us rebels against God. "No one should tell you what to do," he chides us, appealing to our selfish motives.

The reality is that God works through authority. Jesus is Lord; we are not. God appoints those on earth to have authority over us, and as long as they do not require us to disobey God's commands, we must obey this God-ordained authority. We can never be "masters of our own fate" or "captains of our destiny" on any level. We may like to think that's the way it is, and Satan will certainly suggest and stoke such ideas. But ultimately, God is in charge of the entire universe, and we only have the choice to listen to Him and obey, or reject Him and rebel.

Though the lie "I'm in charge" is the primary tool Satan uses to separate us from God, he suggests other lies about ourselves. Most of them attack our worth. I remember the lies Joshua had accepted. At age thirty, he was fired from his position as a staff member of a significant Christian ministry. He crossed some boundaries of modesty with young men who were receiving help from the ministry (no physical touching took place) and was dismissed. Joshua was sent to my office to be spiritually restored because his reputation was destroyed, and for other reasons he could not return to his former position.

The story of how Joshua reached that juncture in life is not uncommon. His father was emotionally distant and worked two jobs.

His older brother molested him before puberty. His mother was young and ignorant about certain aspects of child raising and became irrational at times. Joshua grew up being confused about his sexual orientation.

In his teens, a sexual encounter with a homosexual adult further confused him, and though he was able to hide his struggle from nearly everyone, it remained fixed in the core of his thinking and emotional foundation. A good physical appearance, along with wit and charm, served to further conceal this tendency. Behind it all, though, stood an emotionally bleeding young man whose life was filled with lies and confusion about who he was. Enclosed in that shell, Joshua managed to avoid detection until his firing.

In counseling we spent several days talking about God, truth, and lies. Joshua believed many deep-seated lies. It took many hours of prayer and counseling before he began to let down the internal walls of self-protection. Due to the former abuse, trust was a huge factor.

When we came to this juncture, Joshua said, "I'm going to have to trust somebody and, Ken, I am choosing today to trust you."

I believe that is very important in a counseling situation. I have learned that I cannot teach someone who doesn't think I like him. And I certainly cannot get to the heart of anyone who does not think he can trust me.

When Joshua committed to telling the truth, I led him to forgive his absentee father, irrational mother, and abusive, hateful brother. It was then that the Lord began to speak to his heart about the remaining bondage and lies in his life. Here are some of the errant beliefs Joshua had:

- that he had created a well-ordered life and should not be accused of wrongdoing.
- that the only way people would love and accept him was for him to keep up the masquerade.
- that the only way to be accepted was to appear to be larger than life and at times defiant in a subtle way.
- that his days were numbered. The Lord would certainly kill him while he was young.

As we talked, Joshua told me he lived in a fantasy world. He imagined himself being born with a shroud of mystery around him. He fantasized that wherever he went, people would be drawn into this shroud. When he stepped into a room, something magical happened.

I showed him that the enemy used his fantasy world to keep him in bondage. We discussed the truths that contrasted the lies above. At first, Joshua fought the idea that he was believing lies. He honestly thought his charm and deceit were friends when they were really enemies.

In time, Joshua repented of his fantasy world and all that went with it. He committed to being honest without airs and to daily humbling himself before the Lord. With glad tears of repentance, Joshua whispered, "Lord, I do now choose to tell the truth and to believe the truth. I covenant before You that I will live in accordance with the truth of Your Word and I will reject the lies of the enemy, which include any fantasy."

Today, Joshua meets with an accountability partner on a weekly basis. He is growing in the grace and knowledge of Christ, and he is learning to speak the truth in love.

STRATEGY SIX: Lies About Personal Holiness

A sixth way Satan lies is to tell us we can never grow in personal holiness. God's command is, "Be holy, for I am holy" (1 Peter 1:16). But Satan deceives us, saying, "You can't be holy, you're too weak. Give it up" or "God asks the impossible. He doesn't expect you to live up to this principle" or "Real spirituality is only for the most committed and knowledgeable Christians. You should simply be content with what you already have."

The truth is that God wants us to grow into the likeness of Christ, becoming truly holy—separated from all sin—as much as possible. It's not that He expects us to become sinless, but as I've heard it said, He does want us to sin less and less and less.

An example of this is David, who as a believer was addicted to Internet pornography. His wife caught him viewing filth on the Internet at home late one night. She confronted him and he came to see me about his addiction. In my presence, he prayed what sounded like a prayer of repentance. I helped set him up with an accountability partner through his local church. This appeared to work until we discovered David merely hid his sin deeper, so that it was harder to catch him at it. He quit viewing pornography at home but began doing it at work.

In effect, he lied not only to his wife and accountability partner, but also to God. One day, though, he was caught in the act and, as a result, lost his job as an engineer. It was at that point that he came to see me again and brought his accountability partner along. This time I saw a truly broken man who wanted freedom from his sin.

Once again, we set up a process of spiritual disciplines that his partner would question him about weekly. David, now seeing the consequences of his sin—which I believe God had "engineered" to bring him to real repentance—began to take seriously his situation. He listened to his wife and his counselors, and in time he became completely free of his lust for pornography.

Satan told several lies that David believed. The first was that he could worship God and also worship pornographic images. A second lie was "No one will find out, so what's the problem?" A third one was "It's a harmless thing. What's the big deal?" A fourth seemed to let him welcome the temptation: "You cannot live a holy life in every area. God does not expect you to become holy in this area." As he said bluntly to me during one counseling session, "The positional holiness spoken of in church was to me simply pie-in-the-sky thinking. If God really expected this level of holiness, He would have created me with fewer male hormones."

Pornography led David into an ever-deepening whirlpool of sin. Because of his addiction and sense of helplessness ("I can't avoid it; that's who I am"), he became spiritually apathetic. He lost his enthusiasm for the things of God. He even faked repentance in my office to get me and his wife "off his back."

Ultimately, though, all of Satan's lies were exposed and terminated. God, all-knowing and all-seeing, disciplined David and broke him. God showed him he couldn't worship pornography and also God. He proved that though humans might not know about David's sin, God still did and it mattered to Him. Finally, God demonstrated that there were terrible consequences of his sin: the loss of his job. The truth quickly convinced David that even more serious things would happen if he didn't own up to his sin and turn from it. It was then that David cried out to the Lord and repented of his sin in reality. He was truly set free.

In Part One, we have looked at the nature of spiritual warfare and key strategies of the deceitful and powerful enemy. All of this could easily lead you to believe you are in desperate straits. How can anyone defeat such a powerful enemy?

In the following chapters, I will show you that not only is victory over our enemy possible, it is assured. We'll look at how to wage effective spiritual warfare and we'll see that God ultimately has everything well in hand. It's my hope you'll be inspired not only to get into the battle without fear, but that you will see clearly how to please your Lord and defeat the devil at every turn.

BEYOND THE DECEPTIONS

PART ONE

1. Do you believe Satan is real?

2. Are all of your thoughts your thoughts? If not, what can you do about intruding thoughts?

WE HAVE
A FRIEND

THE GREAT DECEPTION...
AND THE TRUTH

SATAN'S LIE: "God is not your friend. He may be your enemy." (See Job 2:9.)

GOD'S TRUTH: *"There is a friend who sticks closer than a brother"* (Proverbs 18:24).

CHAPTER FIVE

JESUS WAS TEMPTED

Jesus is not only our Savior from sin; He is our Savior from ourselves. Through Him we find the right tactics, guidance, and words to counteract the lies of the devil.

In spiritual warfare, it's easy to get off track, to think we're alone, out there playing the Lone Ranger, and it's up to us to succeed or fail. For the Christian, the greatest truth of all in such warfare is that we're not Lone Rangers and we're not alone. Jesus is with us in every trial and every battle, ready to offer counsel, help, and power to overcome. Through Him we'll learn in the next few chapters the proper and effective way of dealing with the lies of the enemy.

JESUS' TEMPTATION IN THE WILDERNESS

One of the high moments of spiritual warfare in the Bible occurred when Satan tempted Jesus in the wilderness. The story is found in Matthew 4:1–11; take a look at it now.

As we read the Scripture passage and understand its inputs, we learn one of the greatest truths in fighting the enemy of our souls: Our friend Jesus has fought Satan before in every possible way, and won!

This event on the spiritual warfare calendar in Jesus' life occurred shortly after His baptism. Matthew says that the Holy Spirit led Jesus into the wilderness "to be tempted by the devil" (Matthew 4:1). Note that this happened after the wondrous "mountaintop" experience of Jesus' baptism when the Holy Spirit descended upon Him and God spoke from heaven in the presence of John the Baptist and his disciples (see Matthew 3:13–17). Undoubtedly, this grand moment inspired Jesus, much as a "mountaintop" moment can instill new passion and resolve into our lives today. But that's the danger! Satan often strikes at the moment when we've achieved a great victory for the kingdom of God. Just when we're about to celebrate, Satan begins firing his flaming arrows.

Over the years, I have counseled many Christians who have suffered the most grievous attacks just days after major moments in their lives: a conversion, rededication, great ministry, and the like. So it was with Jesus.

But in this case, note that Jesus was "led" by the Spirit into the wilderness for the specific purpose of being tested. This says to me that God the Father wanted Jesus to experience the same kinds of temptation all His people go through at times. This is so that we can be sure Jesus has "been there" and thus can offer us stout counsel when we're in the midst of the battle.

At the Father's direction, Jesus fasted for forty days, going without food or water. In that respect, the enemy dueled with Jesus at His weakest moment physically, mentally, emotionally, and spiritually. Jesus stood on the edge of starvation. That brought with it all kinds of discomfort, anxiety, and distress. When a person is hungry, he or she often loses focus and becomes obsessed with the hunger, barely able to think about anything else. The one who has fasted will often grasp at anything that will slake that hunger and thirst. Satan knew Jesus was more likely to be vulnerable at that moment than any other, so that is the moment he chose to sling his best stones at Him.

Why did the Father put Jesus in such desperate straits?

AN IMPORTANT LESSON

In spiritual warfare, our worst time is always the enemy's best time. He studies us to expose our points of vulnerability. He looks for the chinks in our armor and always fires his sharpest arrows there.

Thus, striking Jesus at His weakest moment physically was not just Satan's strategy; it was God's, too. God the Father put Jesus in the absolutely worst situation. Why? Because by being in the worst circumstances possible, Jesus can then help any of us in our circumstances, which certainly could not be worse than His. Remember, Jesus was not only tempted to be proven, but also so that we could know He understands precisely what we're facing—having gone through it Himself—and thus find in Him real help. This gives us the power to trust Him without question, an essential outlook in any form of warfare. (Remember Joshua in the previous chapter? His breakthrough came when he began to trust me, his counselor, and God, his Father.)

GRATIFYING *OUR* DESIRES

So where did Satan fire his first dart? In an area I like to call "selfism," those issues that involve satisfying and gratifying ourselves without considering God or His purpose for our lives at that moment. As Jesus stood in the shade of a rock in the barren, steaming wilderness, Satan probably hovered nearby. Looking healthy and well fed, the tempter pointed to a stone at His feet and said, "If You are the Son of God, command that these stones become bread" (Matthew 4:3).

Here we see some most revealing elements of Satan's normal attack strategy:

1. Goad the person into taking personal action, to accomplish things by himself. He started with a sarcastic put-down designed to prod Jesus into action. "*If* You are the Son of God," Satan began. That was a deliberate attempt to motivate Jesus to prove Himself. Which of us hasn't been goaded into doing something evil to "prove" we're not "goody-goodies" or to

show we aren't afraid of some little thing the Bible calls sin? How many young people have turned to drugs because someone said, "Prove you're man or woman enough," or tough enough, or cool enough? So it is that Satan often appeals to our pride in order to get us to take other sinful steps that could lead to disaster.

2. Urge the person to accomplish something easy to do. The first temptation involved something Jesus could easily do. While no normal person could turn stones into bread, Jesus possessed that power. Similarly, Satan always tries to get us to do something we can do easily and even effortlessly, even though we know it's wrong. This is why the temptation to steal in a time of need, lie in a moment of exertion, or commit other sins in tight situations often looks like the "easy way out." Satan wants it to look that way because then it won't seem so "bad" to do. And even if you give in, you can give a supposedly reasonable excuse: "I just didn't see that much wrong with it!"

This is the strategy Satan frequently uses with us. He appeals to what he can do or would like to do, so we can accomplish the goal. What were the real issues at stake here? First, would Jesus obey His Father in a seemingly trivial matter (not eating until given the go-ahead)? Second, would Jesus' sense of pride make Him take the quick, sure way to show who He really was, or was He willing not to defend Himself and let God take care of that matter?

For us, similar temptations arise whenever we:

• Feel compelled to defend ourselves in wrong ways.
• Think obeying God in a little thing isn't that important.
• Believe we should take matters into our own hands instead of waiting on God's timing.

The actual sin, of course, occurs when we give in to those feelings, thoughts, and beliefs.

Jesus countered Satan's suggestion with a deft quote of Scripture from the book of Deuteronomy: "Man shall not live by bread alone; but man lives by every word that proceeds from the mouth of the Lord" (8:3). Jesus didn't reach for common sense, public opinion, or even the modern findings of the "experts," the Pharisees and Sadducees. No, He went straight to the best source of all, the Bible, chose a verse appropriate to the situation as a source of guidance, quoted it, and obeyed it. That's a very simple procedure any of us can easily follow. It also reveals how important it is to know and apply God's Word in dealing with the enemy.

A SECOND TEMPTATION: LET GOD DELIVER YOU

The second temptation concerned Jesus flinging Himself off the pinnacle (highest point) of the Temple in Jerusalem. Satan used the "If You are the Son of God" goad again, and then added that God would send His angels to catch Him before He struck bottom. Again, we see a couple of elements in Satan's strategy:

1. Goad more. If at first Satan doesn't succeed, he'll try, try again.
2. Quote Scripture. Perhaps Satan figured that if Jesus wanted to use the Bible then so could he, even though what he said was slightly out of context and left out certain words. This may indicate a subtle trick on his part, or a cavalier attitude toward Scripture; both were probably true.

But what was the real temptation here? It was the issue of trust. Would Jesus trust His Father implicitly, or would He "test" His Father by doing something to force God into action to protect or save Him?

We are similarly tempted when we consider doing the following:

- Take wrong action rather than wait on God in a serious matter.
- Tell God we won't believe in Him unless He does something we consider important to "prove" Himself.
- Do something that is probably wrong because we believe God really wants to help us and will forgive us anyway.

This happened with Abby, a single woman who had prayed for a husband for many years. All through Bible college she prayed, "Lord, please bring Your choice of a husband to me." However, Mr. Right never showed up. Abby entered the workforce and began climbing the corporate ladder. She also became active in a large church. However, she still longed for the contentment she believed a husband would bring to her life. As she entered her thirties, she began to grow bitter toward God. As an attractive, intelligent woman, why would God withhold from her the only thing her heart truly desired?

In the midst of her despair she met Preston. In her words, "Preston was sort of charming and sort of strange." She went on to explain, "The positive thing about him was that he claimed to be a Christian, and he attended church regularly. The negative that I should have seen but overlooked was that he had been through three divorces. More than that, none of his children wanted anything to do with him."

Within weeks after their wedding, Abby said, "I understood why three other women divorced him. He would qualify for Hitler's younger brother." Preston's affair with a high school girl was the final straw that brought Abby to my office.

Abby said, "I gave up on God and decided to create my own life. I really believed Preston would become the loving husband I dreamed of. Instead, I now believe that I know what it means to live a life that is hell on earth." Abby believed the enemy's lie that she could create a kingdom for herself apart from the will of God.

In time, Abby repented of her bitterness and willfulness. Preston repented of his adultery and a list of other sins too long to list. They are still together as husband and wife, and I believe God by His grace will strengthen their relationship. Abby says she has hope. "It will take a lot of work and grace to bring us up to the place where a relationship ordained by God should start."

Abby believed that if she made the jump (got married), God would have to catch her (make the marriage the wonderful relationship she always dreamed of). It didn't work that way.

Jesus' response in the wilderness reminds Abby—and us—of the solution: Draw on the Scriptures for guidance. "It is written again, 'You shall not tempt the Lord your God,'" Jesus told Satan (Matthew 4:7), citing Deuteronomy 6:16.

While Satan "rolls with the punches" and changes tactics to suit his purposes, Jesus is strong and steady, not veering from His successful counterpunching.

A THIRD TEMPTATION:
GET WHAT YOU WANT—WITHOUT GOD

Satan was clearly reeling and frustrated, so he decided to go for the big one. He took Jesus to a mountain and "showed Him all the kingdoms of the world and their glory" (verse 8). Then he said if Jesus would only fall down and worship him, He could have it all.

This was the classic "power play." Satan was "giving it everything he had." This is a pattern in spiritual warfare, too. When you refuse to give in to "lesser" offerings, Satan will up the ante and try to snare you with bigger and better trinkets in his bag, so long as you do it without God. You won't give in to pornography, so he'll throw wealth or power at you. You're not buying that "you're a dope" line, so he'll nail you with an attack on your pride as you overhear someone "commenting" on your skills or integrity.

What was the real temptation here? Satan wanted Jesus to get God's results without following God's plan. Jesus came to take back the ground Satan had stolen—the whole world. In that wilderness meeting, Jesus could have taken it all back in one little act of worship. He wouldn't have to endure the pain of the cross or any of the other indignities He faced at the end of His life. No, He would get the world back for one small genuflection toward Satan. Of course, worshiping Satan meant giving up His soul to Satan, too. But the devil didn't really want Jesus to think about that!

How does Satan tempt us in this way? By offering us something—pleasure, power, wealth, prestige, honor, popularity—through following anything other than God's methods.

That's what happened to Mark, a seemingly successful pastor, yet a shattered man with broken dreams. His story came out in bursts of protracted sobbing. In his words, "As a child I was short, overweight, and not very smart. I worked frantically to earn good grades in college and seminary. After graduation my wife and I were called to a small church in a growing city. I always felt overwhelmingly inferior. Shortly after taking my first pastorate, my older brother came for a visit. He was serving on the pastoral staff of a three-thousand-member church. His parting comment to me was 'You are wasting your time pastoring a two-bit church.'

"I was crushed. I idolized my brother, and his mockery was almost more than I could bear."

Mark then explained how he thought of a plan the very day his brother left. The plan was simple and workable. It unfolded as follows: "You will become somebody when the church attendance reaches a thousand. You will feel good about yourself; your brother will finally accept you. All you have to do is triple the size of the church auditorium, start a Christian school, add a number of new programs, and purchase three more buses."

It sounded rather awesome to me, but it happened. In the next eighteen months most of Mark's dreams came true. "On one 'big day' the attendance was over 1,200," Mark recalled. "My brother and a lot of other people took notice. I was frequently asked to speak on how to build a big church. Finally I had become somebody."

However, this kind of success can carry a tremendous price tag. "I built a monstrosity," Mark said. "The ministry grew far too quickly; I became nervous and driven. The church had become like a huge machine that demanded my constant attention. I was working eighteen to twenty hours a day. I constantly criticized my wife and children. I was blind to what was happening in my own family."

Mark was learning that when we allow the devil to crawl into the vehicle of our life, the Evil One will often say either, "Put the pedal to the metal" or "Put the brake to the floor." Either one can kill you on the freeway of life.

SATAN, THE GOD OUT OF BALANCE

Satan is the god out of balance. "When my wife filed for divorce, I woke up," Mark said. "I snapped out of my dream world only to embrace disaster."

Mark's wife refused to reconcile, and the divorce went through. In counseling Mark repented of taking total control of his life with hardly a thought about God and His will. He began to ponder passages of Scripture that gave him understanding about who he is in Jesus Christ. During one session he exclaimed, "Flesh, flesh, everything I was doing was in the flesh!"

Today Mark works behind the scenes with a mission agency. He raises funds and helps with administration. He is living a balanced, relaxed, and productive life in the will of God.

In contrast, we see Jesus in the wilderness avoiding all the trouble of carrying out personal plans without God. He did so by simply following Scripture. When the devil offered Him everything in the world (as he did to Mark above), Jesus quoted another verse from Deuteronomy (6:13) and said, "Away with you, Satan! For it is written, 'You shall worship the Lord your God, and Him only you shall serve.'"

JESUS' STRATEGY

From Jesus' wilderness temptation we see several elements of Christ's overall strategy for counteracting the enemy during spiritual warfare. First, He relied not on His own common sense, wisdom, or personal integrity to deal with Satan's attacks; no, He relied solely on Scripture. From that we see that a working knowledge of the Bible is essential in our warfare with the devil. The Word of God is the sword that the Holy Spirit uses (Ephesians 6:17).

Second, we note that Jesus actually quoted the Bible aloud to Satan. Even when the enemy's temptations are mere thoughts in our minds, it may be wise to quote the Word verbally to repel a taunt.

Third, and most important, Jesus obeyed what the Bible said. He not only knew it and quoted it; He acted on it. Even the most knowledgeable Christian, when he fails to act on what God has said, sets himself up for failure.

Melissa had come to me because she was struggling with her thoughts. A psychologist diagnosed her with obsessive-compulsive disorder (OCD). Months of therapy did nothing to relieve her condition. As we talked, Melissa explained that she began having thoughts about performing repetitious behaviors after her mother died. Two nights after her mother's death she walked into the house and a thought entered her mind that said, *Turn the light switch on and off twice or someone else will die.* The next day while driving onto the freeway the thought came, *Turn your signal off and on twice or someone will have an accident.*

In time, Melissa became completely controlled by her obsessive thoughts. "I would have an unsettled emotional pain until I would switch, check, and wash everything again and again. Then peace would come, but it would never last."

I explained that the enemy wanted to control Melissa's drives. The enemy was seeking to control her with the lie that she had to do things a second or third time to obtain peace.

This all changed as Melissa learned to combat these lies with God's truth. She later told me, "When I quote appropriate Scriptures such as 'All things are lawful for me but I will not be brought under the power of any' (1 Corinthian 6:12), God's peace does come. As I draw closer to the Lord and verbally take my stand against the enemy, I live in Christ's victory."

Melissa recited the truths of Scripture whenever such obsessive thoughts came. Through such verbal "stands," Melissa learned the power of the Word in her daily battle with the enemy. As a result she no longer suffers from OCD.

What is the lesson here? Scripture, rightly used, is a powerful weapon against lies; it declares the truth to us and to the accuser of our souls. This is what Jesus did during His three temptations.

When we follow Jesus' example, we are following someone who has "been there" and found the Word of God reliable. Jesus, the friend who sticks closer than a brother, is the source of our hope and insight.

Temptation is not the only area of spiritual warfare that Jesus can help in. In the next chapter, we will see another area where Jesus gives comfort and His peace.

CHAPTER SIX

JESUS
KNEW
SUFFERING

W hen the going gets tough, the tough get going." That's one way
to look at times of hardship; pull yourself up by your boot-
straps and move along. Hang in there. Or there's another way to look
at difficult times of suffering and setback: "God works out His good
purposes in our lives through unjust difficulties we endure." That's
the biblical way of dealing with suffering and problems of this life (see
Romans 8:28).

Be assured: Anyone who follows Christ *will* experience pain and
suffering. The suffering comes at the hands of the devil, our own
sinful practices, and the world itself. It's part and parcel of what it
means to serve and love Christ in a sinful, lost world bent on following
falsehood.

Nonetheless, though Scripture clearly warns us of suffering, persecution, and illness in this world, the devil perverts this truth by
telling us that we should never suffer or go through hard times as
Christians. If we are, it's only a sign we don't have enough faith, or

that we've sinned in some way, or even that God is angry with us for some reason and is punishing us.

Counselors see Christians in a steady stream who believe their emotional and spiritual problems are a result of sin, when in reality they're often a result of the lies of Satan meant to stymie and subjugate them in spiritual misery. What is the truth about suffering—mental or physical illness—and how does it relate to spiritual warfare and Jesus as our first and final friend?

First, recognize that all Christians, even those walking closely with God, can and will suffer. The great deceiver will tell Christians that they should never suffer, be ill, or experience deep pain if they're living a committed Christian life. This teaching is prevalent and common in the church today, even from respected teachers and preachers.

The problem with such teaching is that Jesus Himself provided ample proof that this cannot be true. He experienced every kind of persecution possible during His life and on the cross was subjected to the worst forms of torture, mental and physical. Yet He certainly had no lack of faith or spiritual sin that could account for His troubles.

ABOUT OUR BODIES

We should also realize that much of the suffering we have from physical and emotional disorders is not the result of unbelief, worry, sin, or failure to trust God. We have human bodies that malfunction. At times we need medicine and the help of doctors. A psychiatrist can often help people with "mind" sickness—not mental illness, but a sickness of the thoughts and mind that debilitates them emotionally and spiritually. It's true that psychiatry, like other sciences, contains truths, half truths, and pie-in-the-sky fantasies. But with Spirit-led discernment, there are times when we must seek a competent psychiatrist's or psychologist's help.

A common example is found with clients experiencing psychosis. I have seen psychotic believers who, after being prayed over for weeks, go to the hospital and with proper medication function with a clear mind in forty-eight to seventy-two hours.

This is also true with more common maladies like depression, anxiety, food disorders, obsessive-compulsive disorder, and many others.

ABOUT GOD'S WONDER-WORKING POWER

But say you have no problem visiting doctors or believing that Christians, like everyone else, will face real suffering in this world. It's here that Satan provides an opposite lie that is just as sinister. He spreads teaching that says there can be no supernatural physical healing in this present age. These preachers and teachers do not believe God heals or can heal today, and thus they and their followers rely only on human intervention. This can be as sinister and evil as calling on God alone for healing and forsaking all medical help.

In these matters I find that balance is needed. On the one hand, God tells us that suffering happens to all in this world for many different reasons. It can't be avoided. On the other hand, God encourages us to seek Him when we are ill, for He is capable of supernatural healing and does so in some cases. It's possible to have a biological brain malfunction that has nothing to do with demons, faith, or obedience to God. Frequently, medication or some kind of chemical therapy heals these people quickly and completely.

Extremism is Satan's byword. But through our friend, the Lord Jesus, we can find the balanced way to real peace.

SUFFERING CAN BE AN OPPORTUNITY TO GROW

What about suffering? Is there any benefit to it?

Absolutely. Suffering is often God's way of perfecting us. Hebrews 5:8 tells us that Jesus learned obedience through the things that He suffered. James wrote that suffering leads to endurance, which results in maturity in Christ; therefore we should rejoice in it (James 1:2–4). Thus, much suffering has redemptive value.

But what about the mental and emotional suffering we've been discussing? Is that suffering also redemptive?

Once again, Jesus our friend sets the pattern:

- He experienced suffering of all kinds so He could identify with us and we would know He understands our plight (see Hebrews 4:15–16).
- He learned obedience through suffering (see Hebrews 5:8). God

brought Him to human maturity not through memorizing a few truths, but through a day-by-day process of learning to obey even when it didn't seem to make sense.

- He promises to be "with us" in the midst of our suffering (see Isaiah 41:10–13). We never need fear being alone.

One of my clients I'll call Robert demonstrated the redemptive aspects of suffering after he came to me in deep anguish. As a child, he suffered harsh discipline and even abuse. This led him into the homosexual lifestyle. He told me that because of his long-term childhood abuse, "I rejected God's ordained gender for me. I believed I was a woman trapped in a man's body. I considered myself to be an abomination to God rather than a son."

He often called himself a "sideshow freak" and didn't think God could possibly look on him, let alone love him. Over time, he grew into an adult who sinned habitually in the homosexual lifestyle, breaking the commandment of God. He told me, "The sin in my life led to emotional withdrawal and attempted suicide. This put me in the hospital many times where I suffered hopeless thoughts and feelings, convinced I was incurable."

The idea that he was truly a woman in a man's body was actually reinforced by counselors, psychiatrists, and hospital staff. One Christian psychiatrist told him he was hopeless and should simply reconcile himself to his condition. He kept trying, but real purpose, love, peace, joy, hope, and faith eluded him. He was deeply depressed and suicidal when I began to work with him.

Robert's freedom came through a process. He and I met one hour per week for a year. Each time we met I would ask him to give me a report about what the Lord was teaching him through the Scriptures that week. One session Robert exclaimed, "Jesus really likes me. This past week He said that to me through His Word." He reported two passages were especially helpful, Psalm 73:23–24 and Isaiah 58:11.

BELIEVING THAT GOD CAN HELP

For the first time, at age forty-five, Robert began to believe God could help him, and even do the impossible of enabling him to overcome his obsession with feeling like a woman inside. He began to see that nothing was impossible with God. He told me later, "I believed the lies that my problems were far too great for the Lord and that I was so wicked that the Lord would never want to have a relationship with me."

Satan had bound him in a terrible prison of lies that could only be broken by the truth of God's love and Jesus' fellowship in his sufferings. He entered a steep battleground, but at the end emerged whole and renewed.

The strangest part of the story is that Robert's father was a pastor and denominational leader. For years, Robert saw his father's religion as superficial. Inside the home, the father was angry and abusive. The effect on Robert was that he believed salvation was something external, never reaching the inner man. I spent much time convincing him that Christ cared about everything in his life and that He wanted to be a part of every aspect of his life, to transform him into the image of Himself.

One day, Robert gave me a letter in which he described the transformation that was underway. It said, in part, "The Lord is repairing the gate of my heart, rebuilding the walls, removing the obstructions to the fountain, cultivating the garden, cleansing the sanctuary, taking His seat in the throne room, fortifying the armory, and filling the treasury. For the first time in my life I have hope. While I cannot say right now that I am fully restored, I am growing in faith and have peace and joy for the first time in my life."

Robert is being renewed in his mind as he lets the Holy Spirit control his life. Robert now knows he is a man and feels he is a man.

SOME QUESTIONS

Using Robert as the example, let's ask some questions:

Did God send suffering to Robert because he was a vile sinner? No, he was a child when these things began happening.

Did God inflict him because God ceased to love him? No, rather He used Robert's suffering to lead him to Himself and to that love.

Did God tell Robert he didn't have enough faith? No, instead God led him to real faith.

God used Robert's suffering in a redemptive way. Robert was responsible for his sin before God, yet God did not condemn him, but rather used that sin to bring conviction and lead Robert to real faith and a real relationship with Him. Through Jesus his friend and counselor, Robert saw that his suffering had a purpose in the eyes of God. It was profitable and good for him, not something to be ignored or brushed over as worthless pain he should strive to escape as soon as possible.

THE CITY OF REFUGE

It's in this context that I often tell my clients about the biblical idea of a city of refuge (Numbers 35:9–28). In ancient Israel, if a person killed another person by accident, the offender could run to a city of refuge. There he would be safe from avenging relatives. He had to stay there, though, until the death of the high priest, but the offender always had some hope when caught in a horrible circumstance: God gave him (and other transgressors) the city of refuge to protect innocent people from sinful avengers.

In the same way, Jesus is our city of refuge. In Hebrews 6:18 we read, "We ... have fled for refuge to lay hold of the hope set before us."

Just as each city of refuge was chosen so that every Israelite would be close enough to flee to one when necessary, so Jesus is near to all who call upon Him. He is the true friend we can trust in every circumstance.

A client I'll call Marty had his life changed when he ran to the city of refuge. He called me one day and was direct. "Dr. Copley, my daughter told me to call you. She works full time with a Christian ministry. She thinks you can help me. My problem is I am a chronic alcoholic. I would love to become born again, but I think I am an atheist. My wife became born again two years ago, but no matter how hard I try I can't believe."

I met Marty the following week, and he said he was still an atheist. I took him through the gospel. He understood it quite well, on account of his wife and daughter testifying to him. In the process I told Marty that Jesus was our high tower and refuge.

"You can run to Him and be saved," I said, explaining the idea of a place of refuge for the lost.

"I would love to do so, but I'm not sure I have enough faith," Marty answered.

I believed the enemy was trying to deceive him about faith. I knew he had faith; it took faith for him to call me, faith to come to my office, faith to seek the Lord. I asked him if he was willing to put his imperfect faith in the perfect work of Calvary. He said he was and he did.

It happened so quickly, I almost had to ask for a replay! But it was real. The concept of the city of refuge hit the mark, and Marty understood this was what Jesus was in reality.

The change in his life was radical. Marty said, "For the first time in my life the Bible speaks to me. I now read the Word with understanding. One night I was tempted to drink again. I ran to Jesus for help and He was there. It was as if He reached into my heart and took away the desire to drink. I am so thankful to be His child."

Jesus truly became Marty's city of refuge.

Once again we see the power of Jesus to be our friend in suffering. But that's not all. In chapter 7, we see another way He can help us.

CHAPTER SEVEN

JESUS
IS A
FAITHFUL
FRIEND

Joan showed up at my office desperate and scared. Before she came, she had explained that she heard condemning internal voices and felt hopeless and worthless. She added that she was addicted to alcohol and wanted to die. When she walked into the counseling room, Joan began with this disclaimer: "I'm an agnostic." The look on her face as she told me this said, "I have really been wounded by someone religious."

After some get-acquainted chitchat, I said, "Would you entertain a 'what if' question?"

"Of course," she said.

"What if there is a God?"

She said, "I am very uncomfortable with that statement."

After talking for a time about the possibility of the existence of a supreme being, I asked permission to go a step further. I asked her, "What if there is a God who is a personal God?"

"That thought frightens me!" she exclaimed.

A PERSONAL GOD?

This resulted in a thought-provoking discussion concerning the possibility of a personal God. I then asked if I could take the discussion one step further. She agreed. I said, "What if there is a personal God who loves you?"

"That's impossible!" she retorted.

I sensed something deep and possibly horrible lurking beneath this outburst, and I asked more questions, probing her and waiting for honest answers when she deliberated. Soon, a floodgate of emotions welled out. She exclaimed, with a level of intensity I rarely see, "I grew up in an evangelical home and was taken to church on a regular basis. At the same time my parents were engaging in drunken orgies in our home."

As she described her childhood experiences, I began to understand the horror lurking inside. Joan had been exposed to the most vile sin and abuse at an early age. As a result, she grew up confused and cynical about religion and God. The god of her parents was a dirty joke. She recoiled at the thought of knowing such a god.

In further conversations I was able to present the living and true God, citing specifically the character and person of Jesus. Using many Scriptures, I showed Joan four truths about the caring and vibrant life of Jesus of Nazareth:

- Jesus came down from a perfect home in heaven to a sinful earth not only to show people how to live abundantly, but also to make it possible for them to have that abundance in reality (from John 10:10).
- He gave up all His possessions in order to identify with men and women and be like them so that people would know He truly understands their plight (from Hebrews 2:17–18).
- He purposely chose not to show His glory to people, but was like them in every way, experiencing poverty and pain, rather than glory and power (from Philippians 2:6–8).
- He became a servant to those around Him, even to the point of washing His own disciples' feet so that He could show them He was not only willing to put them before Himself, but to

set an example for how they were to behave toward others as well (for example, Luke 22:27; John 13:3–16).

Through these truths, I was able to show this counselee that Jesus is the God who prays for me, weeps with me, loves me, lives in me, and serves me.

Joan was astonished at these revelations, finding them attractive but difficult to accept. When we finished, I asked, "What will you do with the true Jesus?"

Joan didn't know and continues thinking about that question. Not all counseling situations lead to a conversion, and I continue to pray for her salvation.

"CHRIST IN YOU"

"Christ in you [is] the hope of glory," wrote Paul the apostle in Colossians 1:27. Christ in us is the first step to victory in spiritual warfare. For those who are reading this book and live without Christ, realize that faith in Jesus Christ is a vital piece of armor—the helmet of salvation—that we put on to withstand Satan's attacks. (See Ephesians 6:17; we will learn more about the helmet of salvation and other articles of spiritual armor in chapter 10.) When Jesus becomes our Savior, the deliverer from our sins, we enter into a relationship with God that, among other things, makes us "children of God" (John 1:12).

"If anyone is in Christ," the Scripture says, "he is a new creation" (2 Corinthians 5:17). The transition from being outside of Christ to in Christ often has amazing consequences. A person can literally "change overnight" from being addicted to a life of sin to being free to serve Christ in a new and holy lifestyle. This is what happened to Charlie.

He called me out of desperation. He said his problem placed his marriage and his job on the line. He went on to explain that he was employed as a hospital administrator and that he was using drugs. He had tried to quit many times; however, he would always return to them during times of pressure.

His question was to the point: "Is there any power on earth that can set me free from this hell I live in?"

I told him I believed there was, and he made an appointment. We sat down with an open Bible, and in a matter of ten minutes he received Christ. He left my office beaming. He then read through the entire Bible in the next two weeks, and he and his wife became active in a local church. No longer addicted to drugs or any other artificial stimulant, Charlie says, "When Jesus saved me, He also delivered me from drugs. I have never used them again; moreover, I have no desire to do so."

Sometimes God in His wonderful grace instantly sets a person free like that.

OUR FRIEND IS OUR LIFE

In the classic hymn "What a Friend We Have in Jesus," writer Joseph Scriven asked, "Can we find a friend so faithful, who will all our sorrows share? Jesus knows our every weakness, take it to the Lord in prayer." Jesus, the "friend who sticks closer than a brother" (Proverbs 18:24), is one with us in the battle against Satan.

Jesus is particularly powerful when people despair, even to the point of thinking about suicide. Satan uses suicide as the ultimate strategy to stop someone from loving, serving, and knowing Christ. Indeed Jesus said this thief, Satan, comes "to steal, and to kill, and to destroy" (John 10:10).

On numerous occasions I have sat up all night with someone who wanted to take his life. Typically, when a person reaches this point, he or she has lost all hope. To have real hope, one must believe that "help is coming even though I'm at a crisis point." When a person loses all hope, believing that no help is there, was there, or will ever be there, the individual considers suicide.

To help such people realistically takes more than fine words or a list of things to do. The only real workable answer is to connect this person with the One who can give hope, our friend the Lord Jesus. When a Christian despairs of life, the only answer is to reconnect him with the great love of the Savior who laid down his life for his friends (John 15:13), and to the truths of His Word—that He accepts us fully, as we are.

OUR FRIEND GIVES CONSOLATION

That's how Anna found consolation. In the twenty-four hours before I met her, she tried to take her life twice. Her father had ridiculed her appearance as a teenager; she told me in our first session that her father, who loved to read lewd magazines, "would frequently walk into my room while I was getting dressed and make fun of my body. Often, he would hold up the centerfold from a pornographic magazine and say, 'This is what a real woman looks like. It's too bad you are not a real woman.'"

As Anna wept about the things she was telling me, I could see the emotional pain from that abuse was overwhelming for her. She said, "I felt dirty, trapped, hopeless, and abandoned."

Her father's obvious addiction to pornography affected her relationship with men. Anna ended up marrying a man who had the same addiction as her father. She married him at age sixteen to get away from her father; but in less than two years, this man left Anna for another woman.

In time, Anna married a second man who on the surface seemed different. He seemed to be living a victorious Christian life. He loved and accepted Anna and invested his time and energy in their children. All seemed to be going well until one day Anna found several pornographic magazines her husband had hidden in the basement.

She said, "My world was shattered. The feelings of rejection were devastating. I felt wretched and hopeless. Once again those awful feelings of extreme shame and inadequacy swept over me. My father's awful remarks about my body rang in my ears. I was tormented by the thought of my husband comparing me with the women in those magazines. I asked myself, 'Why does he need them? Why am I not enough?' I could not bear to look in the mirror. I loathed the person God had 'miscreated.' The only way out was to take my life. The mental torment was unbearable. I was desperate to die."

It was at that point that the impulse to suicide began to take hold. She tried several times and failed, as is typical among women who face this type of abuse. She came to me with little hope of ever seeing the light of day again. But as we talked, my heart went out to her and after hearing more of her story, I began to talk her through some Scriptures about God's view of us as His people and as His personal creations.

Anna had come to believe many lies of Satan, including:

"I am worthless."

"God made me ugly."

"No one loves me or could ever love me."

"The only way out is through killing myself."

We talked in depth about these lies and what Scripture said about them. One day, Anna revealed a major change had taken place in her heart. "I saw that the Lord totally accepts me as I am. He, by design, created me the way I am."

After so many sessions trying to see God's truth, something had broken through! At that moment, I too felt joy in her discovery. She continued, "I am beginning to understand that my father's remarks were lies. The shape of my body does not determine my value and worth. His wicked comments were really slander against my Creator."

I asked her about her husband's situation with pornography, and she said, "The Lord showed me that I was not the cause of my husband's problem with lust. It was a choice he was making. I always blamed myself for his sin. Sometimes in the past, I would repeat in my mind, 'I am fearfully and wonderfully made,' as you told me. But sometime in the early morning hours, the Holy Spirit brought the truth of that verse to my heart. God enabled me to thank Him for my body. For the first time in my life I was able to accept myself as the Lord has made me."

In a moment, Anna had come to a riveting truth. Christ had broken through the wall of lies Satan had built in Anna's mind, and light shone through like sun through the eye of a hurricane—only the hurricane was over.

"Peace has replaced the torment in my soul," she told me later. "The enemy on occasion tries to bring back the old lies and feelings, but I have found that standing with Christ and resisting the enemy with truth causes him to make a hasty retreat. I know now I am truly a child of God and my identity is found in Christ."

Anna is just one of many women I know who experienced the torment that results from deep feelings of inadequacy compounded by their husband's addiction to pornography. Without the Word of

God and the power of Christ, I personally would have had no ability to help her. But Jesus truly is a "very present help in time of trouble" (Psalm 46:1).

By the way, pornography is a monumental battle zone for many Christians; it's not just nonbelievers who struggle with this snare from Satan. I believe the problem begins with wrong attitudes of dissatisfaction with God's provision in their lives through their wives.

Many men and even women enslaved to pornography and all the sins that go along with it begin to think there is no way out. Their marriages get worse and they may even end up divorced as Anna did. But as a counselor I can tell such people that our friend, the Lord Jesus, can cleanse us from all immorality. When we walk in Him and let Him live in us, we can begin day by day to live free of our lust and sin.

OUR FRIEND IS FULL OF MERCY

Jesus, the Son of God, is a friend full of mercy, just as His Father is. He is ready and able to restore those who have fallen deep in sin, whether from pornography, substance abuse, even murder.

Earl sought such forgiveness after one life-changing evening. Earl was drunk; he knew it was wrong to slip behind the wheel of his dad's car. Moreover, his license had been revoked a month earlier when he was arrested for, yes, drunk driving. When his seven-year-old sister begged to go for a ride with him, even in his drunken state he was aware the answer should have been no. Earl says he doesn't remember running the red light and he has no memory of the truck hitting the passenger's side of his father's car. However, he says he does remember the gurgling sound his little sister made as she died before the rescue crew could get her out of the car.

The eighteen months Earl spent in prison gave him a lot of time to think about his actions on that tragic day. He was in my office several days after his release. The most astounding thing for Earl was what I told him about Jesus—that all could be forgiven in Him through faith.

Earl said he was amazed that "Jesus died for my sins, my rebellion, drunkenness, and my responsibility for the death of my baby sister. All of that was paid for on the cross."

He knew he didn't deserve deliverance for his sinful actions, but that's what Jesus offers all who come to Him confessing sins and inviting Him into their lives. He gives grace and, in withholding ongoing punishment, He shows mercy. That day Earl asked and received the forgiveness of our heavenly Father. He invited Jesus into his life. His joy was heightened as he realized he would see his sister once more. He told me that his sister had trusted Christ as her Savior one year before the deadly accident. "She's in heaven now, waiting for me. I know that one day I will see my sister."

Such faith nearly always brings tears to my eyes. But it also reinforces in me the power of Christ's forgiveness. Through it, we can gain real peace.

This is another reason I believe Christian counseling is the only kind of counseling that can truly work. Christ's forgiveness is the reality that opens the door to all the other truths about Him.

OUR FRIEND IS HOLY AND LOVING

Jesus is called the "Holy One" in Psalm 16:10. God tells us, "Because He is holy, we are also to be holy" (see 1 Peter 1:15–16). God has called us to be holy (pure and blameless) and like Jesus in every way.

Nonetheless, this offers another place for the great deceiver to spin his atrocious lies. How does he do it? By equating holiness with keeping rules. He drives us to do religious things, and he is quick to tell us that if we do just a little more God will accept us. This is the essence of "legalism," a false doctrine that says keeping a list of dos and don'ts is the way to become acceptable to God.

For many Christians, this system becomes a monstrous burden that they cannot carry. Some give up. Others become judgmental and hypocritical, condemning everyone who isn't practicing the same laws they are, whether it be wearing their hair a certain way, saying prayers at certain times during the day, or attending certain church services "without fail."

Satan is the father of this legalistic, performance-oriented, burnout-for-God belief that permeates many churches.

We need to understand that true holiness comes by obeying God out of love. Indeed, He calls us to obey Him out of restful love relying on grace to empower us. Jesus despised the legalists during His days on earth. He confronted the greatest legalists of all time, the Pharisees, who had helped devise and enforce hundreds of laws for holy living that even they didn't keep, but pretended to. They had become classic hypocrites, saying one thing in public and practicing another in private. They commanded all Jews to embrace their system of legal holiness. One of Jesus' greatest invitations was to come out of this burdensome system of false religion. In Matthew 11:28–30, He said, "Come to Me, all you who labor and are heavy laden, and I will give you rest. Take My yoke upon you and learn from Me, for I am gentle and lowly in heart, and you will find rest for your souls. For My yoke is easy and My burden is light."

In this classic statement, Jesus proved for all time that He was not a legalist. He offered us rest and freedom, not a long list of dos and don'ts.

Yet, many Christians come to me out of such a system, pleading for relief. I am only too happy to point them to the true friend of friends, the One who can make us holy only through the power of God.

As a professional woman who dressed well and radiated confidence, Lynn looked supremely elegant and in control. In my office, however, as she related how as a child her mother was never home, she wept uncontrollably. The reason: Mom was always working for the church. Her mother often said she was "frantically seeking acceptance by the Lord" and that was what drove her to do so much around her church. Unfortunately, this led Lynn to feel deep rejection by both her mother and God—she had not done as much for the church as her mother had—as well as feeling unloved and unlovable.

As we studied Scripture together in my office, these "lies" were dispelled, and not only did this lady find acceptance in Christ, but she also was able to forgive her mother.

Another lady told me how awful life was after she "lost her salvation." Her sin: She remarried after her abusive husband divorced her. Because of some hard and legalistic teaching she'd heard in her church, she believed that her second marriage constituted perpetual adultery. Her pastor told her, "Adulterers all end up in the lake of fire when they die."

This is not an uncommon teaching in the church today, and it disables many Christians emotionally and spiritually. I was able to offer this lady some straightforward scriptural teaching on God's grace and mercy, as well as what constituted adultery and divorce and how God's forgiveness for even the worst cases was always available.[1]

As she read the truth of Christ's forgiveness and compassion in her own Bible, her assurance of salvation came back, and through that the Lord confirmed that He loved and accepted her. She told me later it was the most life-changing experience she'd ever had.

In my estimation, legalism is the greatest battleground for deceiving Christians today. We have to remember that it is not merely hard to live a holy Christian life; it is impossible! Without the filling and power of the Holy Spirit, no one can possibly please God. No list of rules and trying to keep them (and failing) can generate real holiness. But through the Spirit, the power to live out God's real rules becomes resident inside us. We can please God as we walk in the Spirit. We will follow the rules because they're written on our hearts, not on our Bible flyleaves.

OUR FRIEND IS GREATER
THAN OUR UNDERSTANDING

Still another truth about Christ as our friend comes from the arena of spiritual understanding and comprehension of God's plan. What about the circumstances of life and when bad things happen to "good" people?

Frequently, the Lord does things that stretch my understanding of who He is and how He works. But in Christ we gain the ultimate picture of God: not an answer man, but a man who answers when the need arises. His answers, though, are not always what we expect. He gives us the wisdom and power to deal with our troubles; He does not always tell us why the troubles happened in the first place.

For good reason Sally could not understand why men had raped her many times during her early teens. But an abusive father participated and even permitted it (by his friends), and a passive wife, fearful of losing her marriage, ignored it. Even Sally's older brothers had attacked her. The anguish of Sally's vain attempts to resist, of the physical and emotional pain that followed, showed in the tears pouring down her cheeks as she described the horrors. Now in her forties, her life felt shattered. She wanted inner wholeness from the very depth of her being, but that wholeness seemed to elude her.

What I am about to say is something that doesn't often happen until several counseling sessions have taken place. It's also something that most counselees rebel against deeply. I never offer it lightly, nor as a panacea that will supposedly cure everything. But at times, I see it as the essential ingredient for spiritual health. It's the issue of forgiveness. I've already talked about this several times, but in many cases, the thing separating a Christian from God's peace is a simple act of forgiveness, wiping the slate of an abuser or tormentor clean. That's not to give the offender an easy way out, but to lead the counselee to find true freedom and to honor God by keeping His command that we forgive others.

I have never found an easy way to say it to anyone, because often the horrors some people have perpetrated on others are truly unconscionable. But that is probably why forgiveness is the only way out—because no amount of restitution, confession of sin, or "doing good to make up for the bad" can rebuild a wounded soul.

As my counseling session with Sally progressed, I decided to open up the issue of forgiveness. In Sally's case, one of her abusers was her father. I knew this would make forgiveness especially difficult. But I tried to say as gently as I could, "I believe the only way you can truly find freedom and peace in the midst of this atrocity is to forgive your father first."

Sally immediately screamed, "I can't forgive him; what he did was too awful!"

FORGIVING AS JESUS DID

After I calmed her down, we talked about this at length and her response remained the same. I wasn't sure what to do, but she knew Jesus and I did, too. I have learned in such situations that having Jesus at our right hand is the greatest source of help, hope, and healing. He is truly the "Wonderful Counselor" of Isaiah 9:6. Thus, in counseling, I sometimes just try to introduce the counselee to (or remind the counselee of) this friend. With Sally, I stopped and simply prayed aloud, "Lord Jesus, please show my sister how she can forgive those who have so deeply wounded her."

I have seen Jesus care for such people in a deeply tender and personal way beyond anything I could conjure up with words. In the moments that followed my prayer, the Lord spoke to Sally's heart and directed her attention to the wonderful truth that He understands us even when we don't, as He did with Paul in the story of the thorn in his flesh (see 2 Corinthians 12:7–10).

Sally told me in that instant light seemed to flood her heart, and she saw something in her mind's eye that opened her spirit to this truth. She said, "Jesus showed me His cross. I was hanging on the cross with Him and those who abused me were standing around the cross. In my spirit I heard Jesus say, 'Father, forgive them for they know not what they do.'"

Her voice broke and she said, "I knew then that because I was crucified with the Lord Jesus, I, in Him, had the ability to forgive all of those people."

It was a remarkable picture I know only God can give, but I have seen it in counseling many times. Christ our friend gives us just the right piece of wisdom and strength to do what must be done.

It was then that Sally, by God's grace, could forgive—every one of her abusers. She told me, "As I forgave my abusers, God's peace and joy rushed into my heart."

She hadn't been able to do it on her own willpower, but as the power of the Holy Spirit and her new understanding of what Jesus did on the cross filled her mind and heart, she was set free. Jesus became Sally's Jehovah Shalom, "the Lord is peace."

I have found over and over that even when we don't completely understand the reasons behind certain pain in our lives, Christ can open our minds and give us His understanding. That is often all we need.

SOMETHING MORE

Something else happened in the counseling room that day. As Sally vividly described what the Lord was showing her, I also gained a new understanding of the Cross. I saw that because I am crucified with Christ, I have the same ability (through the power of the Holy Spirit) to forgive others as Christ does. When we forgive, we defeat Satan's grasp upon us through fear and bitterness.

It's almost shameful to admit, but sometimes my counselees offer me the very counsel I need to solve a problem in my life. Prior to my session with Sally, there was one person whom I could not forgive. I had prayed, released, and scripturally done everything I knew to do from a counseling standpoint. Yet there was still some bitterness in my heart toward this person. As Sally quoted Jesus, "Father, forgive them for they know not what they do," it was as though I suddenly understood forgiveness on a new level in my heart. I spoke the words in my soul, "I forgive, Lord," and with astonishing force the bitterness melted away and a new love for this person took its place.

I have found that God burns biblical truth into my heart by trials, pressure, meditation on the Word, and time. That day, the Holy Spirit used a vivid picture of the cross to do a permanent work in the depth of my being. It's amazing it works that way, but I can tell you with real fervency that it is true. Jesus can even work in a methodic and calculating counselor's heart now and then!

Remember, this battle we have entered is terrible. There are casualties on every side, and sometimes it seems as if Satan is winning on every front. But the greatest source of strength, understanding, personal integrity, holiness, and victory is there, in Jesus our friend of friends. He promises to be there no matter where we are or what we're facing.

That is to me, both as a counselor and as a Christian, the bedrock truth of fighting back the forces of evil in this world. Truly, without Him, we can do nothing. But with Him, nothing is impossible!

BEYOND THE DECEPTIONS

PART TWO

1. Have you placed your trust in the finished work of our friend, the Lord Jesus Christ?

2. Are you walking with the Lord in a growing love relationship?

WE HAVE
THE TRUTH

THE GREAT DECEPTION… AND THE TRUTH

SATAN'S LIE: "Truth is relative and can be found only in yourself." (See Romans 1:25; John 18:38.)

GOD'S TRUTH: *"I am the way, the truth, and the life"* (John 14:6).

CHAPTER EIGHT

THE POWER
OF THE TRUTH

My spiritual life is dead. I've lost contact with God. I feel like I'm running on empty." I knew Larry was serious about his problem. He had waited four months for an appointment, and then he and his wife drove six hours to reach our office. After I opened the session with prayer, those were the first words out of his mouth.

Larry could not understand why his spiritual life felt so empty. He began telling me about all the "right" things he was doing: "I get up at 4:30 A.M. I power walk six miles, shower, pray for an hour, spend time with my wife and children, go to work, come home, pray with my family after the evening meal, spend time with my wife and family, and go to bed."

He went on to explain how he was a trustee at church, did mechanical work on church equipment, drove the bus to pick up elderly people, and so forth. I almost got worn out just listening to him. I thought to myself, "There is nothing like a good example. With discipline like this he is going to ruin it for the rest of us! After all, God doesn't grade on a curve." (The fact is, God doesn't grade at all, but at that point I was too stunned by this man's obvious spiritual prowess to think about that.)

But he had not mentioned one element, so I decided to ask a question. "Larry, do you ever read the Bible?"

He gave me that "deer in the car headlights" stare. After what seemed several minutes, he said, "No, I don't."

His frantic life included hours in prayer but no time in the Word of God. I explained to Larry the dangers of all prayer and no Word. "Larry, prayer apart from the Word can lead to mysticism." I went on to show how the Scriptures are foundational to our relationship with the Lord.

"My brother, without the nourishment of the Word, you are starving spiritually," I explained.

"No wonder I have dried up spiritually," he replied. "I have been deceived."

I further explained how the Word and prayer can't be separated. I warned him of the danger of getting out of balance. Reading only the Word is one way the enemy keeps us off center. Reading the Word without prayer often leads to legalism and its offspring, coldness of heart. Praying without spending time in the Word leads to a reliance on "spiritual" feelings. Larry had fallen into the second trap.

Larry is now reading the Scriptures, praying the Word, and growing in Christ's likeness. He still gets up at 4:30 A.M., and when I'm around him I'm still a little worried that if God looks too hard at him and then me, I might be in trouble. But I'm still glad he has restored balance to his life by reading and reflecting on God's truth, the Scriptures.

Spiritual warfare can be best understood as God's truth against Satan's lies. As believers we have the written truth, God's holy Word, and the living truth, Jesus Christ. In this section we'll see the power of God's truth in contrast to Satan's lies and how that truth can be used for the battle and for overcoming the enemy in a falsehood-loving world.

THE TRUTH ABOUT TRUTH

The solution to any lie is the supernatural illumination that comes from the Holy Spirit and the holy Word of God. Only truth can dispel a lie. But what is the real power of that combination, the Holy Spirit and the holy Word?

Jesus revealed it in a few words from John 14. The disciples of Jesus had been shaken by His revelation that He would soon leave them (see John 13:33–37). For three years, He'd lived with them, eaten with them, spent time with them, as some say, "24/7," meaning twenty-four hours a day, seven days a week. These men had left their jobs, homes, and security to follow Jesus. And now He was leaving them! The disciples were terrified. What would they do? Where would they go? They'd put everything they had into the life and times of Jesus Christ. Now, seemingly, He was leaving them stranded!

It was then that Jesus brought out the greater truth, a truth that would truly make these men invincible: He would give them another comforter, the Holy Spirit. "But the Helper, the Holy Spirit, whom the Father will send in My name, He will teach you all things, and bring to your remembrance all that I said to you" (John 14:26).

Through the Holy Spirit, Jesus is with us, in us, going ahead of us and behind us. The Holy Spirit is our resident comforter, teacher, encourager, and friend. He's Jesus living in us. It's perhaps the greatest truth of the Bible: Wherever we are, Christ is. We cannot be anywhere that He isn't.

Through the Spirit of God, Jesus takes what is in the Word of God and makes it practical and effective in our lives. He answers our questions, shows us how to deal with difficult situations, and guides us through the "valley of the shadow of death" when necessary. In spiritual warfare, that valley can open up before us and seem to swallow us before we even know it. But with the Spirit in us, we cannot fail.

THE TRUTH ABOUT LIES

By now, you can see the real power of the lies of the enemy. Lies are his greatest weapon. The degree of control he exercises over us is proportional to the lies we believe. The more lies we believe, the more the enemy will control and enslave and destroy us.

The lies can come from anywhere: the attitudes and beliefs of society, what coworkers and friends say, our parents, even our own minds. Satan uses them all to try to defeat us. The solution is to know the truth about God and us, found in Scripture.

A lie had enslaved John, a good father who loved the Lord. He was serving on the pastoral staff of a growing church. The Lord had blessed him with a wonderful wife, great children, and much fruit in his ministry. John's major problem was his weight. He had been grossly overweight since his preteen years. Many times he had joined various weight-loss plans and several times lost close to one hundred pounds. Within a short time after coming off a diet, though, he had always packed the weight back on.

The strange thing was that John exercised tremendous discipline in all other areas of life. He maintained a rigorous spiritual life. He led in his ministry most effectively. His wife and children were happy and committed to their lives together. So why couldn't John control his eating habits?

In counseling I asked the Lord to bring to John's conscious mind what lie the enemy was using to drive John to eat so out of control. The Spirit of God illumined John's mind and as we talked and prayed together, he recalled a traumatic event and saw quickly its relationship to his eating problem. "I was molested sexually by a teenage boy my parents kept for foster care. He would put a knife to my throat and molest me. Then he would threaten to kill me if I ever told anyone. This went on from the time I was six years old until I turned eight. At that time the foster boy turned eighteen and left our home."

It's astonishing to me how many lies Satan fixes in the minds of Christian people. They often stem from abuse: physical, emotional, and spiritual. But what was the lie Satan used on John? He believed that when he lost weight he would become sexually vulnerable to men. Homosexuals would select him as a "closet gay" and do the same unspeakable acts to him that this foster boy had done years before. Thus overeating became his way to protect himself from future male sexual advances.

This might strike you as strange—why would he think that?—but that's the power of a lie like this. It doesn't have to make sense to anyone but you!

As the Lord revealed that this lie lay behind John's overeating, he gained new freedom over food. He told me, "The next morning

I began to eat my 'normal size' breakfast. I was only able to finish half of it. The powerful desire to overeat was gone."

Today, he continues to control the problem, and he has not experienced advances from gay men.

THE SPIRIT OF TRUTH

I have witnessed such turnarounds numerous times. And yet, in the greater counseling community, I hear over and over that such problems are often so ingrained that most people will never overcome them. Just taking the whole issue of weight loss statistically, the reason so many people latch onto the latest diet fad is because all previous ones have failed. And this latest one will, too. Most dieters spend their lives hopping from program to program and book to book and never succeeding.

Yet, for a person like John, his turnaround happened just hours after the Spirit exposed the real lie behind his problem. What is the source of such power in a believer's life? In a word: the Holy Spirit. He alone can account for showing and exposing the truth behind Satan's lies and so set people free from lifelong problems.

The Holy Spirit lives in every Christian. He is the dispenser, teacher, and illuminator of truth (John 14:17, 26). He is a person. He is not just power or energy in the abstract. The New Testament says He has intelligence, a will, feelings, and knowledge. (See 1 Corinthians 2:10–11; 12:11; and Ephesians 4:30 for proof of His personality.) He has the ability to love and is the very essence of life. He is to be our guide and resident internal source of power, leading us into the truth and into right conduct (John 16:13–14).

MARTHA'S SUNRISE

The Spirit's primary work is in guiding us into God's plan for our lives. I saw the Spirit work in this way in Martha.

Martha, age thirty-five and a believer in Christ, was suffering from deep emotional pain. During a counseling session, I asked the Lord to bring to light the lies Satan had hidden in her inner being. As I prayed, the Lord brought several lies to Martha's mind.

"I believe I am really evil," she soon noted. I showed her then what God actually says about her. "Not by works of righteousness which we have done, but according to His mercy He saved us, through the washing of regeneration and renewing of the Holy Spirit" (Titus 3:5).

Martha thought about this and said, "Then according to the Bible I am washed clean!"

The next lie the Holy Spirit brought to her mind was "God can never love me because I am so awful." I then read the wonderful truth, "We love Him because He first loved us" (1 John 4:19). Her eyes lit up as the truth of God's love for her sank into her heart.

A third lie soon came to mind: "I can never change; I will always be sinful, dirty, and awful." At this time I personalized 2 Corinthians 5:17 for Martha: "Therefore, if Martha be in Christ, she is a new creature: old things have passed away; behold, all things for Martha have become new."

"I must start acting on the truth that I am a new person in Christ," Martha said.

I continued to pray that the Lord would reveal the enemy's lies, and even more were revealed. It was almost as if we were in Sunday school and I was asking a class of children these questions. Except in this case, my class was one, Martha, and not a little child but an adult. And yet, as she sought the truth through the Holy Spirit, the truth shone through in that way Jesus spoke of when He said, "Unless you . . . become as little children, you will by no means enter into the kingdom of heaven" (Matthew 18:3).

As we explored the lies that were more deeply ingrained in Martha's thought processes, she said, "If I serve the Lord, I will never be able to serve people because they will become idols to me." The Lord destroyed this lie through Ephesians 2:10: "For we are His workmanship, created in Christ Jesus for good works, which God prepared beforehand that we should walk in them."

"So a true servant worships God, and part of that worship involves serving people," Martha replied.

The last lie the Lord showed her was "I can't face truth because it hurts too much." A number of Scriptures served here, but I read

John 8:32: "And you shall know the truth, and the truth shall make you free."

It was as if a sunrise suddenly appeared to someone on a desert island. The pain simply melted out of Martha's heart, and she began to reveal the real nature of what she'd endured.

She had been abused beyond description by her parents and siblings. Amazingly, despite the sin in this household, Martha was taken to church every Sunday. During that time, Martha would often pray, "Please, God, make my family stop hurting me."

Yet the most severe physical and sexual abuse would take place on Sunday afternoons, after attending church. Part of Martha loved God and part despised Him. Martha would hear the pastor preach on answered prayer, but then the enemy would whisper, "God doesn't answer your prayer, now, does He?" Another sermon explained the "peace that passes all understanding." Martha would cry out for such peace, but when it didn't come, Satan seemed to say, "You will never have this peace, only pain, because God hates you." Still a later sermon title was "God Can Get You Out of Any Problem." Satan loved this sermon; he said, "Anybody but you, Martha, because you are not worth it."

During counseling, I looked with Martha at Scriptures that described God's good plan to have His children serve Him because He loves and accepts them.[1]

Knowing the truths that God makes no mistakes and uses all things for our good (Isaiah 40: 10; Romans 8:28–29) sets a person free from the past. It frees him or her to walk confidently in the present. Martha is now able to search the Scriptures on her own, and often the Lord gives her special insights. Several times she has explained a passage to me in ways that no one had ever been able to. I often marvel at the wisdom the Holy Spirit gives her through His Word.

The guidance of the Holy Spirit gives us confidence, and His teaching in truth makes our lives truly worth living.

CHAPTER NINE

HOW GOD'S TRUTH WORKS IN WARFARE: THE ARMOR

The Scriptures teach that we are personally involved in spiritual battle. This war will continue the whole time we live on earth. The war ceases when we die. At that moment, the Lord strikes the final victory bell and our homecoming, with a song of triumph, will begin.

Until then, though, the battle rages. Satan's attacks usually are subtle. After all, he is the great deceiver. But his power on earth is considerable, and he can undertake a direct attack on those who give him a stronghold.

I remember, for instance, the day Jonathan came for counsel. Two days earlier, he had tried to take his life. We began our meeting with some friendly chitchat; I sensed a warm relationship developing as we visited. Then I asked, "Jonathan, what sin in your life do you feel the enemy is using against you?"

Jonathan answered, quite honestly, "I am a heavy user of pornography. I believe it is an addiction with me."

He described for me the kind of hold it had on him and many other details about it. I finally asked if I could pray for him. He seemed to welcome the offer. I prayed, "Dear Father, your child has sinned by making a naked human body an object of worship. Please grant him the gift of repentance."

I wasn't expecting anything dramatic, but when I said the word "repentance," the most amazing thing happened: a spirit threw him on the floor as if it were gagging him. I immediately prayed for Jonathan, "Heavenly Father, this evil spirit is harassing your child. Please bind him and set him aside."

At that point Jonathan relaxed and was able to return to his chair. Seconds later, a prayer of repentance and confession poured out of him like few I have heard. In only moments, he appeared free of his bondage. He then asked me, "Do you know why I was thrown on the floor?"

"Please tell me," I said.

"I didn't believe in demonic powers. I thought I could be a Christian and indulge in pornography, and somehow get away with it."

I stared at him, quite amazed. He added, "Today I have become a believer in the existence of the enemy."

I smiled happily at the change and encouraged Jonathan to read the Bible regularly and apply it in his life. He followed that advice consistently. Jonathan's parents later reported to me, "We have a new son, one who loves the Lord and who obeys His Word."

In this case, God let demonic powers drive Jonathan to such an extreme that he finally turned back to God in desperation. Clearly, that was God's purpose all along. The lie in Jonathan's life could only be vanquished by his seeking God with integrity. God had to apply the truth to Jonathan's specific need like a torch to metal. Mere candlelight would not have done anything.

Most Christians will not confront the enemy or his forces so directly. But they will still engage in spiritual battle. The reminder—and warning—from Scripture is that "we do not wrestle against flesh and blood, but against . . . powers, against the rulers of the darkness of this age, against spiritual hosts of wickedness in the heavenly places" (Ephesians 6:12).

The spiritual battle may involve resentment, showing disrespect to authority, jealousy, or even verbal fighting between parents and kids. We need the armor to withstand *all* satanic attacks, including feelings of inferiority, selfish ambitious plans, and attitudes of indifference to those in need. No matter the sin, we need spiritual weapons to confront and defeat it.

NORMAN'S JEALOUSY AND BITTERNESS

Norman worked for a large manufacturing company. By his own admission he said, "I am from the old school and at times I am a little bullheaded." For several years he eyed the foreman job. He knew the foreman would retire at age sixty-five. Norman worked diligently and felt certain the job would soon be his. He arrived at work early, stayed late, and produced more than any man in the plant.

When the big day came to choose a new foreman, though, Norman was passed over for someone much younger; in fact, a recent hire. "They brought in a runny-nose college graduate to do a man's job," Norman told me. Some of the adjectives he used to describe the new foreman and the decision are unprintable. Norman had learned the company chose to computerize some of the machinery as the old foreman retired. That resulted in the need for a man with computer training as well as people skills (which I discerned Norman lacked). Norman became jealous of and bitter toward the new foreman.

His bitterness didn't stop there. He also became bitter toward the Lord. He resigned his Sunday school teaching position, asked to be taken off the deacon board, and quit reading the Bible.

"How do you like those apples?" he said as he finished telling me his story.

I answered his question with a question: "Norman, where is God in all of this?"

I waited in silence for several seconds. Norman seemed to calm down and really think about the question.

"I pushed Him out!" he finally answered.

"Are you willing to invite Him back in?"

He paused. Then with tears in his eyes, he answered, "Yes!"

Norman confessed his sin of bitterness, pride, and desiring control of his life. He then asked the Lord to take back the ground the enemy had been given through his sin. Norman was now willing to reason scripturally. He admitted that he wouldn't fit the foreman job, but he desired the prestige, title, and power he thought it would bring to him. He could now clearly see God's protection in keeping him from getting a job that would lead to frustration and eventual failure.

Norman could also see that what God intended for spiritual development the enemy attempted to use for destruction through bitterness. Norman learned a whole new appreciation for the armor of God.

He says, "My favorite part is the shield of faith. It puts out those burning arrows that Satan shoots at my heart." Today Norman is serving the Lord with a new excitement because joy and peace have replaced the bitterness in his heart.

THE TRUTH IS WE'RE IN THE BATTLE

While God does allow Satan and his demons to "wrestle" with us, that wrestling can always be redeemed, and God is always ready to step in on behalf of a repentant believer. The truth, though, must be applied specifically, not just bandied about in general terms. Like it or not, we *are* in the ring against satanic forces. Every believer is involved in spiritual warfare, even though he or she may not know it.

Spiritual warfare cannot be fought at a distance, as if you can let others do it for you. No, it is hand-to-hand combat.

The way to succeed in the battle is found in the verses surrounding the biblical warning of Ephesians 6:12. The victory is ours if we "put on the whole armor of God, that [we] may be able to stand against the wiles of the devil," if we "take up the whole armor of God . . . in the evil day" (verses 11, 13). The enemy is no passive observer. When we are commanded to "stand against" the enemy's lies, our position is active, confrontative, and direct. Being watchful is the critical element for becoming engaged in the battle.

Many Christians simply avoid or refuse to recognize this truth that they're in a spiritual battle and needful of spiritual armor. Their refusal to recognize the battle is often the thing that keeps them bound in chains to the tortures of the enemy.

How then do we wrestle effectively against this enemy of our souls? We find instruction in Ephesians 6:10–18. Let's look here at the first two pieces of armor, and then in the next chapter at the rest.

THE TRUTH ABOUT THE BELT

In Ephesians 6, the apostle Paul begins the discussion of the armor by describing a belt of truth. What is this? It's our truth system in Christ. "Stand therefore, having girded your waist with truth" (verse 14a).

We are to gird, or encircle, ourselves with four great resources of the truth:

1. Jesus Christ. He is called the truth (John 14:6; 1:14; 8:31–32).
2. The Word of God. Again, it is the "word of truth" (2 Timothy 2:15; James 1:18).
3. The Holy Spirit. He is called the "Spirit of truth" (1 Corinthians 2:10–12).
4. The local church. It is called the "pillar and ground of the truth" (1 Timothy 3:15).

Each of the four resources can help us spot a lie and help us see the truth that will destroy that lie. Whenever the "father of lies" assaults us, the lies will become apparent as we seek Christ, learn from His Word, allow the Spirit to work in our lives, and give the church a chance to speak. Often such attacks are frontal, right at a basic point of doctrine.

Bart and I were talking about the belt of truth in a counseling session. Being desperate for the victory in his life, he took notes as fast as he could. Bart is a medical doctor, so I asked him, "Bart, how are you going to read your handwriting at the speed you are writing?" He laughed and said, "I will get a pharmacist to read it to me."

When I mentioned the church as being part of the belt, he blurted out, "The church has failed." What he really meant was, "The church has failed Bart." He said, "We have church at home, just our family. We watch preaching videos."

I explained to Bart several New Testament passages about the function of the church. We talked about the fact that it is Jesus who builds the church and walks in the midst of the church. I explained that the church represents authority and the church leadership will give an account to God as to how they watched over our souls (Hebrews 13:17).

As we talked, Bart's eyes fell and he nodded with repentance. "I really don't have a true church at home; it was just my excuse for not being part of a local assembly."

Bart saw the lie he had been believing: that the church had failed so he need not be part of it. Bart repented of his rebellion toward God's church and confessed that he had been deceived about the place of the church in his life.

His repentance did not prove empty, either. He began attending a Bible-believing church, took the same kinds of notes he took from me (I don't know whether or not he has to take them to his pharmacist to decipher), and he realizes well the power the church brings into his life, giving his family harmony, friendship, and love. Today, he actively serves the Lord there as an elder and Sunday school teacher. Moreover, he and his family are growing Christians.

Our entire life must be held together by God's truth. When we were saved, the Lord gave to each of us the belt of truth. We all have it. This is the first piece of the armor, and, as a result, it's the first thing we must buckle on each morning. Without truth, Satan's lies will not seem at all like lies, but the way "things really are." That is the subtlety he works toward.

THE TRUTH ABOUT
THE BREASTPLATE

The second piece of armor is equally important, but can be put on only after the truth is accepted and believed. It's called the "breastplate of righteousness." What exactly is this?

This is righteousness that Christ has given to us through His own perfect life. (Theologians call this "imputed righteousness.") The breastplate wards off the accusations of Satan. If the enemy is not foisting some lie off on us, he takes a second stance in which he accuses us. He tells us we're "vile," "foolish," "rejected," and even "hated by

God" because of our sin, bad attitudes, and evil actions. He says we're "not worthy of God's love" and that "God Himself has given up on us."

These are both lies and accusations meant to destroy our confidence and hope in God. Sins and failures provide Satan with much ammunition. God's constant assurance, though, is that if we will confess those sins, He will cleanse us. How can that be? Because of Christ's righteousness. Jesus lived a perfect life in our place. When God looks on us, if we are His children, He sees Jesus and all His goodness, wondrous deeds, and perfection. We are covered with the robe of His righteousness (Zechariah 3:1–5).

That is what it means to put on the breastplate of righteousness. It's not our personal goodness and "perfection" that makes us acceptable to God; it's Christ's. Therefore, when we put on this piece of the armor, we protect ourselves against Satan's accusations. We are righteous in God's eyes because of Christ, not because of our keeping of rules, great acts of mercy, or giving to the church.

What does this righteousness do for us? Ultimately, it means there is no death sentence hanging over us. We are not condemned by God because of our sin, but forgiven and completely accepted by Him (see Romans 8:1). And as Paul wrote, "If God is for us, who can be against us?" (Romans 8:31).

I saw the power of the breastplate of righteousness in Kendra. When I first met her, I thought, "This woman really has her act together. She is single, in her thirties, has a master's degree in psychology, and is the director of a progressive woman's ministry." I really wondered what she was doing in my office.

As her story unfolded, she shared with me that she felt "emotionally crippled." Through a veil of tears she explained, "I accepted Christ in my midtwenties. During my high school and especially my college years I was extremely promiscuous. I've received the Lord, and He is changing my life. Yet I still feel defiled and dirty. I often ask how He can use me. I know the Bible says I am forgiven of my sins, but I don't feel clean."

With tears, she listened as I shared the truth of the breastplate of righteousness and told her, "Today you are righteous. You are as pure and clean as Jesus Christ, because He was the One who cleansed you."

Working deep inside her, the Holy Spirit opened Kendra's heart to receive that truth. She wrote to me later, "That day in your office was the second most profound day in my life. On that day I received in my heart the truth about the breastplate of righteousness, that I have been declared righteous and made, through the blood of Christ, as pure and clean as Jesus Himself. I now know I am clean and I feel clean. The devil has no right to use my sinful past against me, because in Christ I have no sinful past; I am redeemed."

It's a powerful, emotion-filled truth. We are righteous, pure, and clean in God's eyes, now and forever. If I could instantly impress this on all my clients, I would be out of business!

THE TRUTH ABOUT THE ACCUSER

The breastplate of righteousness is an absolute essential in warfare because Satan is truly "the accuser of our brethren" and us (Revelation 12:10). However, he is careful not to accuse us face to face. He uses people, sometimes God's people!

In the years when I was a pastor, I watched more than one "troublemaker" work. They usually had "blessed" other churches in the most subtle and "spiritual" ways by pointing out to the "right" people the flaws of the pastor and church leadership. They are like Diotrephes, "who ... does not receive" what the leaders say (see 3 John 1:9). On one occasion a would-be descendant of Diotrephes opened fire on me. He brought "prayer requests," privately of course, such as "Please pray that the pastor would become more sensitive to the needs of the people." A little investigative work with former pastors revealed that this man always tried to take at least thirty people with him when he left a church. In my situation, he left alone, but only to become a "blessing" to another local church. The devil loves to dress in religious robes.

I have found that Satan accuses us in five ways:

1. *He gets us to accuse and denounce ourselves.* "You're such an idiot. You always do the same things wrong," Satan says. And at times, we agree: "I've got to be the biggest jerk in the universe." Such inner dialogue can truly wound a person when repeated over and over for years.

2. *He uses others to accuse us of past sins or of having wrong motives.* A teacher might tell you, "You'll never succeed." Sometimes even a parent will accuse. "You always were a liar!" said one mother to her daughter.

3. *He works through circumstances to stir up feelings of depression, self-pity, and anger.* We focus on situations in which we have no control or feel we made wrong decisions, and let Satan or ourselves throw accusations. "You can never change your situation." "You brought it all on yourself." Sometimes we look at the injustice of a situation and hear Satan's accusations against another person: "You should be angry. Let him have it!"

4. *He uses doubt.* Even Christians have doubts about their faith; but Satan will cause us to doubt the very nature of God, His Son Jesus, and the Word of God. "How can you believe Jesus was truly God? He was just a man, like anyone else." "God won't work this for good in your life; He doesn't care about you."

5. *He sows seeds of discouragement.* "This is just proof that God is not in this one," Satan sometimes tells Christians. He calls upon them to see God as disinterested or limited and to despair over the situation. "Give it up. You'll never win this situation."

Joe once walked with the Lord. Two things happened that led him to near despair: His wife gave birth to a learning-disabled child, and later he bought a house that had structural problems the inspector did not find before the purchase was made. He became bitter, stopped attending church, and spewed out his bitterness toward God every chance he got. Today, he still accuses God of "messing up his life." In effect, he's only accusing God with the things he hears Satan accusing God of in his mind. It's a primary way Satan works.

THE ANTIDOTE TO THE ACCUSATIONS

What is the antidote to such accusations? The breastplate of righteousness. As we wear it, we hear the truth of God in our hearts each time Satan slings an arrow of accusation at us:

"I am with you" (Isaiah 41:10; 43:1–2; Matthew 28:20b).

"Do not be troubled. I have everything under control" (Psalm 115:3).

"Believe in Me. I'll get you there" (John 14:1–3; Philippians 1:6).

"Don't give up. It's difficult right now, but My plan is working" (Jeremiah 29:11–13; Romans 8:28–29).

As we listen to the truth of God, spoken in our hearts from memorized Scriptures, the Spirit's voice, and friends in the local church, Satan is sent running. His accusations have no power against the truth, so long as we believe the truth and reject his words.

What other pieces of armor must we wear for this daily combat? We'll look at them in the next chapter.

CHAPTER TEN

MORE
ESSENTIAL
EQUIPMENT

One of the most dramatic and critical military maneuvers in the twentieth century occurred on the beaches of Normandy during World War II. On June 6, 1944, American soldiers stormed the shoreline, machine guns armed by Nazi soldiers blazing in their faces. With buddies falling all around, bullets pinging off their helmets, it would have been easy to turn and run. But no one did, and more than three thousand soldiers of the first and twenty-ninth divisions died in the mission.

Two things kept them fighting. The first probably was the fear that the commanding officer would have them shot for desertion. The greater motivation, though, was knowing that they were fighting for a worthy cause, the preservation of the free world. Many soldiers have kept their courage in the midst of battle not because they fear the punishment of desertion, but because they believed in what the war was all about.

For the Christian, though, things are turned around. First, you know you will never be shot for desertion. If you lose your courage, the Spirit of God will draw you back, restore you, and strengthen you so that you eventually learn to face your foe, unafraid.

Second, in spiritual warfare you're fighting not just for America or against the Nazis, but in the greatest battle in world history: against forces of darkness in heavenly places. It's a personal battle that calls for your utmost every day. It's a heroic battle, because you are engaged in performing heroic acts every day. And it's a consequential battle, for it's part of God's plan for history.

Perhaps the greatest difference in a spiritual battle, however, is in the risks and the outcome. For the American soldier in World War II, the risk was great—to his life and the lives of those around him. In addition, he didn't know whether this war would end in defeat and destruction or victory and honor. For the Christian, however, these two things are already decided. No one loses his life; instead each believer gains it, even if he dies in the process. More importantly, the war has been won! Jesus won it at the Cross. (Many verses declare this victory; for example, see 1 Corinthians 15:54–57; Hebrews 2:14; Revelation 5:9–10.) We're just cleaning up the mess at the moment, until He comes to right everything at the end. In that sense, the suspense is less: We still know we're part of the winning team, that our efforts are never in vain, and that ultimately our enemy, even if he fells us now, will be felled himself in the end.

This makes this war utterly worth entering and fighting with all you're worth.

THE SHOES OF PEACE

That is why we can confidently place upon our feet the third piece of armor, the "shoes of peace." Knowing we shall survive, and indeed that Christ shall triumph, allows us to march into battle with inner peace.

Significantly, the Roman soldier wore shoes with cleats on the bottom. These gave him an advantage in battle, for his shoes (sandals) would not slip on almost any kind of turf. Paul chose the image of these shoes to suggest we would be assured and secure when we have this peace. Putting on the shoes of peace meant standing sure in the peace of God.

Thus Paul wrote that we should "shod [our] feet with the preparation of the gospel of peace" (Ephesians 6:15). Such genuine inner peace enables us to stand and walk with a sense of assurance that God is not only with us, in us, and guiding us, but on our side, supporting us and cheering us on. Without such peace, the battle looks endless and overwhelming. But with it, one knows, "God is working His plan and I'm part of it. In the end, all will be well."

How then does Christ's peace work here? Christ's peace in this war sits enthroned in our hearts and functions like an umpire. When we face decisions about serious matters in our lives, we are often drawn in opposite directions. This is where God's peace becomes most helpful, because God gives us peace when our choice, if done in harmony with the Scriptures, is the correct one.

FINDING PEACE

Before I was able to open the session with prayer, my new client Glenn stammered, "I've lost my peace, and I can't find it. Where did it go?"

We began to talk about his walk with the Lord, and eventually Glenn concluded, "I think I lost my peace when I became angry with my new neighbor." He explained that shortly after new neighbors moved into the home next to him, the parties began. The neighbors had big Saturday night parties, Glenn explained. They would rent a hot tub and even an outdoor toilet for their guests. Glenn described the scene. "About nine in the evening their friends would start showing up. By midnight fifty or more people would have gathered to drink beer, dance to extremely loud music, shout obscenities, and throw empty beer bottles into my yard. I tried once to reason with my new neighbor, but all he did was mock me. The next morning all the tires on my truck were slashed."

I told Glenn I sympathized with his plight. Certainly he was bearing a hard load. I have known many people with neighbor problems that continued for years with no respite. It's a difficult circumstance to work out.

However, I also explained to Glenn that his anger and bitterness offended God and grieved the Holy Spirit. I explained that God in His sovereignty had allowed these people to move next door for reasons He had and that would lead to good.

We looked at some passages about loving our neighbors. As Glenn began to agree, he saw the wisdom of simply following God's truth in the matter. With head bowed, he chose to forgive his neighbor and those who partied with him. He repented of his anger and bitterness and asked God to take back the ground he had surrendered to the enemy.

The peace of God flooded his soul.

Now he had a decision to make. How would he respond to his neighbor when the next weekend party erupted? The peace of God directed His steps. Glenn told me later, "The next Saturday evening was party time as usual, but this time God gave my wife and me rest. We slept all night. The next morning I had a song of praise in my heart as I picked up two garbage cans of bottles and trash off my lawn. The next week my neighbor's wife was hospitalized. We sent flowers and a sympathy card. I began to smile and wave at my neighbor, and in time he began to wave back.

"We would always pray for them as a family. At Christmastime we bought them presents. Last summer his wife gave birth to a little girl. At this time the parties abruptly stopped."

As if this wasn't miracle enough, Glenn went on, making me choke up a bit, "Just last week I was able to share the gospel with him. I sensed the Lord was working in his life. He hasn't accepted the Lord yet, but I feel that's coming."

Then Glenn himself choked up and said, "But the greatest work is in my life. I have the peace of God that passes understanding."

The shoes of peace caused Glenn to become a peacemaker. He is learning to love his neighbor as himself.

THE SHIELD OF FAITH

The fourth piece of armor is the shield of faith. This provides confidence in God, that He is good and wise and just and sovereign. We can fully trust Him because He cares, and He assures us that He will intervene in our situation and answer prayer.

Roman shields, which Paul used as the illustration here, were covered with leather. In battle, in preparation for when the enemy shot arrows at an advancing contingent, the soldiers would douse their shields with water. As the arrows struck the shields, because they were made of leather, the arrows could sink in and stick. But their flames could not ignite the surface.

All of Satan's "arrows" can be extinguished by the protection granted by the shield of faith. Paul says, "Above all, taking the shield of faith with which you will be able to quench all the fiery darts of the wicked one" (Ephesians 6:16).

Through the shield we put on the spiritual "eyes" that allow us to see God behind any troubles, and we see that God is working, even in terrible, painful situations. Our firmly planted faith empowers us against the enemy.

PROTECTION DURING TOUGH TIMES

Terry found the shield of faith his ally through a terrible event. Driving home after working the night shift, he saw a cloud of smoke as he approached his street. *That is close to my home,* he thought. As he reached his long driveway, he saw flames shooting above the tree line—from his house. Moments later, to his horror, he learned that his wife and four children had perished in the fire.

Terry told me this terrible story, and I learned he had found Christ as a nine-year-old but soon wandered from God. "During my teen years I sort of forgot about the Lord," he said. "I pushed Him into the background. I married after high school. When our first child was born, we went back to church to dedicate the baby. I promised the Lord I would start reading the Bible and attending church. However, I didn't follow through with my promise. After the birth of our third child I began to realize that God's blessing was upon my life in spite of how I was treating Him.

"At this time I began getting serious about the Lord. Soon our two oldest children received Christ.

"My wife Jan had grown up in a nominal Christian home. Her childhood church did not preach a clear gospel. She believed herself to be a Christian until one Sunday morning the Holy Spirit showed her how lost she was. On that day she went forward to receive Christ at our church. We were growing as a couple and growing as believers. Just when things came together in our lives, she and the children were gone."

So often in situations like these the best thing I can do is listen. What words of consolation can anyone offer? As Paul said, "Weep with those who weep" (Romans 12:15), and that is what I did.

Then Terry added, "I don't understand what God is doing, but I do know the Scriptures tell us to 'set our affections on things above.' I can confidently say all my treasures are now in heaven."

Our session took place several months after his terrible loss. Among other things, we talked about the shield of faith. I explained how the shield keeps us from being destroyed. I explained how as believers, when God in His sovereignty allows one of the enemy's arrows to come through the shield, it is like a refining fire. Even in a terrible situation like the loss of life he'd experienced, I assured him we can trust God, who never errs. We can cling to Him and be confident that He is walking with us even through "the valley of the shadow of death."

Terry picked up the shield of faith and walked on with the Lord, resolving to deal with his grief honestly but also to trust that God knew what He was doing. Now, five years later, Terry has married a fine woman who loves the Lord. They recently adopted a little girl whose first word was "Daddy."

THE HELMET OF SALVATION

The fifth piece of armor is the helmet of salvation. The helmet, of course, protects the head from attack. It signifies the hope of deliverance in trouble and ultimately from hell. It protects my mind from enemy attacks suggesting that I'm not really saved, that I will not make it to heaven, and that God does not love me.

Satan targets our minds here because he knows the power of keeping us unaware of God's truth. If the enemy can control the mind, he can control us. However, if Satan cannot take control of all your mind, he will control whatever he can find. He knows that if you surrender some of your mind today, more will follow. We need the helmet because a wound to the mind can cause serious damage.

Through our minds we grow in holiness, character, love, and faith. That's one reason Paul asked believers to "set your mind on things above" (Colossians 3:2). For us to grow spiritually and have real victory, our minds must be fixed on things above. Only when the mind, heart, and will are working together can we serve the Lord as we ought.

In earthly battle, the two most vulnerable targets are the heart and the head. A soldier who is wounded in either of these places usually dies. For this reason no soldier would go into battle without his helmet or his breastplate on. When we have that helmet on, we:

1. are assured of our salvation;
2. have confidence that death, if it comes, is the door to heaven;
3. know that God ultimately is in control, even if we are not;
4. can trust in God even when things go wrong; and
5. become willing to sacrifice our all for His kingdom.

Melvin found the helmet of salvation indispensable against Satan's attacks. I had counseled with Melvin one hour per month for five years. For several years he had been in the homosexual community, and one day I had the privilege of leading him to Christ. He grew quickly as a new believer; the Word fed his soul as he would grasp large portions of the Bible daily. Melvin said during one session, "I love to bite off a large chunk of the Bible in the morning and chew it all day."

Melvin reconciled with his parents, who had rejected him for his previous sexual orientation, and joined their church. He was warmly received by the members of the congregation and now actively serves the Lord there.

ATTACKS ON OUR MIND

One day Melvin came to counseling with a perplexing problem. The enemy was attacking his mind by saying, "You're not saved. You had a lustful thought about a man, and that shows who you really are. You have lost your salvation."

The great deceiver had clearly planted that thought. As we noted in chapter 4, Satan's number one strategy is to suggest thoughts to us. (Remember Alice, the college junior who thought she was worthless?) When the lustful thought came, Melvin took it captive and confessed it, but Satan still accused him of being a sinner God had not truly saved.

That was when I encouraged Melvin to put on the helmet of salvation each day. As I explained the fact that we are saved apart from any works we might do, I also explained that the helmet of salvation protects our mind from the lies the enemy tries to tell us concerning our salvation. "By the helmet we are reminded that we are delivered from the wrath to come," I told him. "As blood-bought children of God, we are saved from the penalty of sin and the power of sin in this world. One day in heaven we will be saved from the presence of sin."

Melvin grasped the helmet and put it on. Later, recalling our session, he told me, "From that day forward I have put on the whole armor of God daily. The helmet of salvation reminds me that I am secure in Christ because He has won and given me salvation, not because I've earned it. I am truly saved because of Calvary."

The helmet protects our minds, the very point at which Satan most often strikes. Over and over, as I've helped Christians understand this amazing piece of equipment, I have seen them change from saints in a pit to saints with a peace.

THE SWORD OF THE SPIRIT—THE WORD OF GOD

The sixth piece of the soldier's equipment is his first offensive weapon. All previous pieces—the belt, breastplate, shoes, shield, and helmet—are defensive and protective. With this next piece, we actually gain the ability to advance on the enemy and drive him away. It's the sword of the Spirit.

Paul writes, "And take the sword of the Spirit, which is the word of God" (Ephesians 6:17). The term for "Word" here is *rhema,* which indicates the spoken rather than the written Word. That is a crucial distinction. It calls for speaking the written Word to others and ourselves. A word like this has power only as the Holy Spirit energizes it.

How do we gain the power to use the sword of the Spirit in this manner? The primary method is to hide the Word in our hearts, as Psalm 119:11 indicates. I like the psalmist's focus in this verse: "Your word [the best thing] I have hidden in my heart [the best place], that I might not sin [the best purpose] against You."

We must not think of the Scriptures as if they were magical words to chant or shout. Simply reciting the Scriptures without comprehension is meaningless. But when we understand and use them according to their true meaning, they become powerful truths to believe and apply in our lives.

WIELDING THE SWORD OF THE SPIRIT

Jamie has learned the power of wielding this sword of God's Word. She came to my office in a state of hopeless despair. Five years earlier she had experienced a major emotional breakdown. She spent several weeks in a treatment facility for emotional and mental disorders.

When she stabilized, she went home with hope,—really believing the Lord would help her. Jamie told me, "The next four years were wonderful. I could sense the Lord's presence and I functioned quite well."

That was all to change abruptly. "Doubts kept coming into my mind," she said, "doubts about my salvation, God's love, His ability to keep me, and my ability to persevere to the end."

One morning she woke up and sensed God was gone. "He left a huge emptiness, nothing else in its place."

Jamie felt lost, abandoned by God and beyond hope. I was sure this wasn't true; sometimes God uses this sensation to wake people up to the truth that they aren't truly saved. But in her case, I was sure it was an emotional sensation, not a reality. That pointed me to the problem: Many people base their spiritual well-being on how they feel. It sometimes takes hours of counseling to help such people see that emotions are quite subjective and can be affected by many things.

I tried to explain to Jamie that our Christian life is to be obedience-oriented rather than feeling-oriented. This didn't seem to register. The Lord then led me to Philippians 1:6, which mentions God's power to take us from where we are and help us arrive safely in heaven. I turned to the passage and handed her my Bible. I asked her to follow the verses with her eyes as I read, "[For I am] confident of this very thing, that He who has begun a good work in you will complete it until the day of Jesus Christ." I personalized the verse using Jamie's name for "you" and requoted it. Then I asked Jamie, "How long will the Lord work in your life?"

"Until Jesus comes, or I go to heaven."

"Is this verse true?" I asked.

"It must be true," she answered. "It is the Word of God."

Then I asked, "Is it true for you?"

She began to weep as she said, "Of course it is true for me, because God said so."

That opened a window in her mind. She saw for the first time that her salvation and perseverance were from God, not from her. Her protection was twofold: With the sword of the Spirit—the Word of God—she was able to cut at the lie, and with the Word of God she was reminded to wear the helmet of salvation. Indeed, remembering her salvation chased many doubts she had about God's love and His ability to keep her.

Today Jamie knows she is a child of God. She is also confident that the Lord will continue to work in her life. Because she feels it is true? No, because the Scriptures say so. This is now the foundational bedrock for her belief in the faithfulness of God.

PRAYER: A POWERFUL WEAPON

The last piece of equipment for the successful soldier, and the second offensive weapon, is prayer. It's our only means to communicate with our commander-in-chief. Prayer is the means by which we put on the armor. Prayer is also the power that makes the armor work. Paul states that the Lord wants us to be "praying always with all prayer and supplication in the Spirit" (Ephesians 6:18). Complete knowledge of the enemy and using the best of equipment have no value unless the soldier possesses the energy necessary to face the enemy and use the equipment. Prayer keeps us connected to God's power.

People who drift away from God are never prayer warriors. In that sense, the armor offers no help to us unless we are living in a growing love relationship with Jesus Christ. Only as we walk in fellowship with Him do we receive strength and power from Him. Our prayer lives to a large extent define our Christian lives.

A good case of this was Joey. He was plagued with anxiety about his two children. He was age thirty-two and worried constantly that one of them would be badly hurt or die. Only two years earlier, he had lost his only other son in an auto accident. After the death of this three-year-old, Joey's concern for his children became an obsession. The fact that one of his children had died several years earlier stoked his concern and turned it into an obsession.

As Joey and I prayed together, the Lord brought to his mind the fact that he was believing a lie. The enemy's lie was "God really doesn't care for your son and daughter like you do. If you don't constantly have them in mind and worry about them, one of them might die again, or be severely injured—and it will be all your fault." When that lie was exposed, Joey's mind exploded with affirming Scriptures, such as "The Lord is my light and my salvation; whom shall I fear? The Lord is the strength of my life; of whom shall I be afraid?" (Psalm 27:1).

Joey thought about another compelling verse: "Be anxious for nothing, but in everything by prayer and supplication, with thanksgiving, let your requests be made known to God" (Philippians 4:6). Joey knew these verses applied to his children as well as himself. He realized that he had not been taking to his Father in prayer the need of his children's safety. I reminded him that God, who created them, loves Joey's children—loves them so much that He could not take His eyes off them.

Later Joey told me, "That day my life changed. I saw that through prayer I could take my children to the Lord and He would keep them safe in His arms. Each morning I rededicated my two children to the Lord, I asked Him to place a hedge of protection around them, and I have learned to trust Him in a whole new way. Since that day in your office, my anxiety is gone. My children truly belong to the Lord.

"Through prayer I'm constantly reminded of this truth that God loves my children," he added. "My wife and I try to be wise stewards of these precious lives the Lord has trusted us with. But thanks to God; He is their protection."

WEAR ALL THE ARMOR

Author and speaker Warren Wiersbe has reminded Christians of the importance of wearing all the armor. Concerning the when and how of putting on the Christian armor, he wrote, "My own experience has been that the morning is the best time to put on the armor. After I have given God my body, mind, and will, I ask the Holy Spirit to fill me, and then I, by faith, put on the pieces of the armor by prayer."[1]

I cannot think of a better pattern to follow.

BEYOND THE DECEPTIONS

PART THREE

1. Do you love the Person who is the truth?

2. Do you memorize and meditate on the Word of truth?

WE HAVE
A CHOICE!

THE GREAT DECEPTION...
AND THE TRUTH

SATAN'S LIE: "There is no choice; you are an evolutionary product." (See 2 Peter 3:4–7.)

GOD'S TRUTH: *"Be . . . diligent to make your call and election [choosing] sure"* (2 Peter 1:10).

CHAPTER ELEVEN

REAL CHOICES
IN THE
REAL BATTLE

W illie approached me one day as I was leaving my office and said, "Please, we have to talk." One glance told me he hadn't slept well for days. His face was drawn and his eyes were bloodshot.

As soon as we closed my office door, Willie's story unfolded. His father and he had begun a construction company fifteen years earlier. The father was to be the senior partner, but, Willie noted, "everything would be split fifty-fifty. I have worked hard and the company has prospered. The net worth is over a half-million dollars."

Then, Willie explained, financial upheaval came, shaking the company and their relationship.

"My father has recently made some bad investments and he is on the verge of bankruptcy. Last week he informed me that I was fired and the construction company was his sole property. You see, selling the company is the only way he can remain financially solvent. The real kicker is, he not only wants my half of the company, but he also wants the registration to several pieces of equipment that I bought out of my pocket. He now denies that we ever agreed on the partnership. He insists that I was only his employee, and he is threatening a lawsuit if he doesn't get the equipment."

It's amazing what parents will sometimes do to their children. But it's not uncommon. Willie continued, "I am so angry, I kicked my dog and yelled at my wife and children. I can't sleep and I feel like choking my father. What can I do?"

AT A CROSSROADS

Willie was at a crossroads and had to make a choice. He was leaning toward hating his father; already he felt estranged. In his heart he felt his attitude was wrong. But what could he do?

Willie had recognized a biblical principle: Choices begin with our thoughts. Evil always plants its seeds in the thoughts, then nurtures them so that they take root in the heart (James 1:13–15). What we think about, what we meditate on, what we dwell on will determine what choices we make at crucial points during the day. Jesus Himself warned of the relationship. "For from within, out of the heart of men, proceed evil thoughts, adulteries, fornications, murders, thefts, covetousness, wickedness, deceit . . ." (Mark 7:21–22).

How does that work in our lives? If we (as men) look on women, imagining them with their clothes off (or even think of tearing off their clothing) and ravishing them, it's quite possible we could make the damaging choice to commit rape or adultery, look at pornographic images, or even treat our wives as lust objects. Similarly, if a woman envies another woman's fancy clothing, possessions, or attractive husband, this could lead to hatred, ill will, theft, and thoughts of adultery.

Such devices are the tactics of the enemy. He will do anything to build a stronghold in our minds through our thinking.

THE POWER OF WISE COUNSEL

What choices, then, do we have when we begin to have selfish thoughts? How can we respond and resist temptations that come from within and are fed by Satan? That, in essence, was Willie's question.

The first choice is to seek and heed wise counsel. We are not at the mercy of fate, or ill circumstances, or even our own stupidity. No, we can choose, when difficulties strike, to seek out help from relatives, church members, and others. This is an amazingly helpful resource that many people overlook. They say things like, "I have no choice about what to do." Or, "I'm caught! I can't go any way that is good!"

But often, God opens up vistas we never considered, simply by our finding wise counselors—friends, pastors, or even actual counselors like myself. Rarely does God allow situations to come into our lives in which there are virtually no options.

COUNSEL FOR WILLIE

When Willie looked at me through bloodshot eyes and asked, "What can I do?" I admit that my first response to his predicament was to close my eyes and shake my head. This was difficult.

Sitting up in my chair, I questioned Willie on his ability to support his family. He was happy to report that the day after he was "fired" by his dad, he started another job with a ten-dollar-per-hour increase in pay.

"How much are peace of mind and the ability to sleep worth to you, Willie?"

"Priceless," he answered immediately.

I thought of Willie's buying equipment for the company and of his father threatening a lawsuit. Then I chose to remind Willie of the following words of Jesus: "If anyone wants to sue you and take away your tunic, let him have your cloak also" (Matthew 5:40). I explained that there has been misapplication and abuse of this verse, but I believed it applied in Willie's case. I even suggested that Willie sign over an extra trust to his father—which he said he no longer needed —to fulfill the "let him have your cloak also" part.

Willie pondered, prayed, and then called his wife and explained the proposal. She wholeheartedly agreed this was God's will.

Willie forgave his dad, repented of his anger and bitterness, and signed over the equipment. The peace of God poured into his heart, and the love of the Lord was reestablished in his life. Today Willie is happy, his wife and children live in a peaceful home, and even his dog is grateful.

Willie's father's health broke in less than a year, and he is confined to a nursing home.

What was the devil's lie in this situation? The great deceiver had said, "Willie, fight for what is yours. You earned it. Don't back down; you have a right to be angry and bitter. *Get* your dad." In contrast, God's truth was "Seek first the kingdom of God and His righteousness, and all these things shall be added to you" (Matthew 6:33).

Willie confronted the temptation to "get" his dad. True, he has not regained the money he lost, but he has kept his peace, his joy, his life, and his walk with God. What could be more precious than that?

ANOTHER CHOICE: OUR FOCUS

After choosing to receive counsel, another arena in which we have true choice is our focus. We can choose to focus on others. Satan desires that we focus on ourselves. In spiritual warfare, we often find the battle joined because we are tempted to please ourselves.

Kevin began talking before he came through the doorway. "My wife is bitter toward me to the point where she even quit reading her Bible."

As his story fell from his lips, his previous statement began to make sense. A job transfer sent him to a state where his wife for years had longed to live. He was the first to relocate to the area and look for a house to buy. He found what he thought was the perfect house; he had his wife fly in to look at the home, and she fell in love with it. In her mind she had already arranged the furniture when he suddenly had a change of mind. He decided it would be better to rent a house and look around for a while. After a year in a rental home the house sold out from under them. For the next three months they split up the family with relatives while Kevin looked for another rental house.

As Kevin and I talked, what became most apparent was the fact that he had raised expectations in his wife's heart and then shattered them. He had "sold" her on the idea that this dream house would be where they would live out their lives. I quoted the proverb "Hope deferred makes the heart sick" (Proverbs 13:12). I also told him that he was responsible to honor his wife.

In this case, his refusal to provide a decent home to live in was dishonoring to her. As I spoke, the Lord brought to his mind other times he had done the same thing. His marriage was marked by broken promises and looking out for himself.

The Holy Spirit led Kevin to repent of his sin and later to ask his wife's forgiveness. They went house hunting the next week. She is now a content woman in a house that meets her family's needs. He is a happy husband who has the respect of his wife.

The enemy's lie was "You can change your mind and she will understand. It won't matter what you promised her; after all, you are her leader, and your wishes rule." God's truth is "He who swears to his own hurt and does not change . . . shall never be moved" (Psalm 15:4–5).

CHOOSING HOW TO RESPOND

A third arena in which we have real choice is how we respond to the daily situations of life. Many Christians exclude God and make terrible decisions when the circumstances of life intrude on them. Our lives can go from wondrous to disastrous in a moment, and we do not respond well.

A parent has died. You've lost your job. You've learned a good friend is dying of cancer. How do you respond to such tough developments? Many Christians choose to respond by blaming God. They feel that God has "messed up" their happy lives like some kind of divine grinch. Thus, when they face trouble, they have a true choice: to go God's way or their own.

Some people refuse to go God's way, saying, "His way isn't practical" or, "It doesn't make sense." Some argue, "God's way is too hard." Thus, they reject God's directive. They exclude or ignore God in their decision making. You can be sure Satan will jump in at that point with his own alternative.

How can we move in the direction of choosing God's answers for our problems? Through doing two things I've emphasized in this book: knowing God and talking to Him daily.

Almost every client I have counseled did not know who God truly is. The enemy had distorted their perception of who God is; he still does that. In fact, every lie of the enemy is a distortion of either God's Word or His person. Furthermore, most clients I've counseled did not have a prayer life. People who drift away from God are never prayer warriors. They have replaced dependence on God with self-sufficiency, thinking they are masters of their own destinies—a big lie of the enemy that leads to prayerlessness.

To counteract such lies, I try to help counselees build into their lives two resources: (1) a knowledge of who God truly is, and (2) a dynamic prayer life. As we lay this twofold foundation, God fortifies us for the day of battle.

The harsh situation you may be in may not be your choice; but your response is. The truth is that we have a choice about how we react in every situation. We can choose to trust God or blame Him; we can go His way or our way. But we are never "forced by circumstances" into some action. We can and must choose to trust God.

Carol's problem reflects the unwillingness to let God control her life because she did not know Him well. She struggled with a sleeping disorder for twenty years and eventually ended up in a mental hospital, diagnosed as being schizophrenic. A doctor placed her on antipsychotic drugs, but after years of medication, another doctor said she was misdiagnosed; she had a bipolar dysfunction.

When Carol changed churches, she learned her root problem might be spiritual. She told her minister about her treatments and the changed diagnosis. "My new pastor shared with me that mental illnesses may be real, but sometimes they are the result of harboring sin, bitterness, etc., in one's heart."

At that point this pastor referred her to me. Carol waited several months for an appointment, and during that time the Lord began working in her life. Before her visit she sensed God leading her to a number of verses. One from Deuteronomy 10:12 was an eye-opener: "What does the Lord your God require of you, but to fear the Lord your God, to walk in all His ways and to love Him, to serve the Lord your God with all your heart and with all your soul."

During our first session, Carol was open and revealed her childhood experiences of sexual abuse. Carol felt justified anger toward the people who had hurt her and believed that anger, a form of revenge, was right. In the process of our sessions, God revealed this lie the Evil

One had placed in her heart. At first, though, she struggled. Because of her childhood abuse, she felt a deep-seated anger toward God.

In time, Carol forgave her mother and a number of other people. She repented of her anger and hatred toward those who had offended her. And she repented of her anger toward God and for doubting God's willingness to keep His word. The morning after our session in which she'd expressed and done these acts, Carol later told me "My time in the Word was sweet, God gave me a special verse. 'Many a time they have afflicted me from my youth; yet they have not prevailed against me'" (Psalm 129:2).

"The next day revealed that much of my life was based on performance," she added.

For a long time, however, Carol felt I spent too much teaching time on this issue and she became angry. But that night, a providential event was to occur. She went to church and the preacher said, "When you are under pressure the real you comes out. Your choices reveal what you really believe. True repentance results in a change of heart, not just some modification of your behavior."

Carol sat there stunned. Had the real Carol shown herself in her seeking to perform for God? Was doing things to impress Him what mattered to her? Was control the thing she always had to have in order to feel safe?

That night, Carol repented of wanting to control every situation. She sensed God's forgiveness and for the first time she felt truly free. She had learned to accept doing things God's way, not her way.

Later she wrote me about what she was learning through her times in the Scriptures and prayer: "God is teaching me how to die to self and surrender to Christ daily. I am learning in a new way that God is sovereign and in control. . . . I have learned to allow Christ to live His life through mine. The Lord will continue to enable me to overcome bitterness and anger in my life. Praise God, for only He could set me free."

Carol saw for the first time that following God's way through her Scripture and prayer time fulfilled her. By submitting to Him, she would enter into His plan and live out the reality of life in Christ that she had always wanted. I marvel that God's Word and power can cause such amazing changes in a person's life.

WE MUST WATCH AND PRAY

A fourth arena in which we have a real choice is the choice to stop and pray when events churn out of control.

Kent is a perfect example of this problem. When he arrived at my office he was more than simply troubled; he was afraid for his life. He had drifted away from the Lord through neglecting prayer and the Bible. Saved as a child, he knew the Lord was real, but because he was not grounded in a good church, he didn't grow as a believer. When he met Sue in college, he was swept away with her sweet charm. The fact that she was an unbeliever didn't deter Kent from pursuing her with all his heart.

One year after they were married her uncle offered Kent a "job" with the "firm" he worked for. Over the next five years Kent made over $20,000 per week as a major drug distributor. He also became involved in money laundering; his keen mind and expert administrative skills made him a natural for such "work." As the money rolled in, Kent purchased a major nightclub and rode in a stretch limousine.

At times, he felt grieved in his spirit; he responded by drinking and engaging in a sexual affair. At that point his marriage began to fall apart. Late one night Sue tried to take her life, and Kent began to wake up and took a look at his life. Meanwhile, a godly woman took an interest in Sue and invited her to a ladies' Bible study. In time Sue received the Lord.

One evening as he was traveling home, the police pulled Kent's car over. He was arrested on suspicion of committing murder when the gun used in the murder was traced to Kent. (Kent owned the weapon; it had been stolen from his home two days earlier.) Kent said, "That night was the longest night of my life. Around 2 A.M. I began to pray. I hadn't prayed in years, not seriously anyway, but that night I told God if He would come to my rescue I would turn my life over to Him, lock, stock, and barrel." Which, in Kent's world, could be taken literally!

God heard Kent's prayer that night. Through an anonymous tip the real killer was arrested. The new suspect confessed to stealing the gun and using it to take a life. Kent was free. God chose to answer this sinner's prayer. And Kent did recommit his life to Christ.

Kent's story is highly dramatic, involving much money and murder. God, of course, can answer any sinner's prayer—deliver him or her from any problem, big or small.

When he was released from jail, Kent told Sue of his prayer and God's answer. She wept as she explained to him that she was now a believer in Christ. Within days Kent approached his "employer" and told him he was leaving the "firm." This was extremely dangerous, as anyone would understand who has read books like John Grisham's *The Firm*.

Within hours, a bullet shattered the windshield of Sue's car while she was driving. A message left on his answering machine informed Kent that he needed to rethink what he was doing, "or else."

As I prayed with Kent, completely at a loss as to how to counsel him, the verse "Agree with your adversary quickly" (see Matthew 5:25) came into my mind. I said to Kent, "Go to your employer and ask him what it will take to be released."

Kent wanted out desperately but didn't want to jeopardize his family. So he visited his "boss" and laid out his situation. He shared Christ with him, then he asked what it would take to get out alive. His boss made it simple: "Everything you own."

Kent swallowed a large dose of pride and financial worry and decided God's way was better than his way. He signed over the club, his home, and several other investments. His "boss" allowed him to keep all household furnishings and one car.

Kent told me, "I signed over in excess of three million dollars in property, but I gained my freedom."

I was reminded of the verse "What will a man give in exchange for his soul?" (Mark 8:37).

Today Kent and Sue live in a three-bedroom home. Their two children are well adjusted. Kent and Sue walk with the Lord and serve Him faithfully. Their story in its entirety would make a great book. Kent says when the time is right, he wants to write it. For now, though, he is "content in the Lord."

What was Kent's sin? He had vexed his righteous soul because he was in the midst of a group of wicked people. The devil's lie was "Kent, you're a smart, gifted man. You can have anything you put your mind to." The truth answered this thought with a question: "But at what price?"

What price are you willing to pay to gain freedom, truth, love, peace?

Aren't they worth "everything," as Kent discovered?

CHAPTER TWELVE

YOUR CHOICES AND GOD'S POWER

Marriage has its tensions. Each partner may at times fail or wound the other. But love will forgive. Lonnie and Jane were about to learn that as they stepped into my office for counseling.

"I don't want to be married anymore," Lonnie said during our first visit, with Jane seated nearby. I had seen Jane a year earlier and was able to lead her to the Lord. She had become a growing believer and was committed to staying in the marriage. I'd known about Lonnie's feelings through his wife; now I responded to Lonnie's statement by asking the question "Why do you want a divorce?"

"Because she did two things that I am angry about. She told me she planned to leave me two years ago, and she said nasty things about my children."

This was Lonnie's third marriage. As we talked, I felt led to show them Scriptures about repentance, confession, and forgiveness. I could see that his wife was in distress but really didn't know what to do. I also sensed that despite Lonnie's strong words earlier, he really didn't want a third marriage to go belly-up.

As we talked, his wife asked for forgiveness about the things she said that had hurt him. Immediately, Lonnie granted it. Often it doesn't happen this way; many times forgiveness is a process one must meditate on, talk through, and finally reject or accept. It is a choice each person must make—a choice that comes only through the supernatural power of Christ within.

"Well, I don't really want a divorce; I want help," Lonnie finally said. "I feel like a scared little boy inside. I'm afraid others will laugh at me. I don't know how to receive or give love. I need help."

This admission led to Lonnie and me meeting one hour per week in a counseling/discipleship relationship. Since that day he chose to forgive Jane, we've talked about many issues in his life, and I've shown him appropriate Scriptures. Amazingly, he can now pray with his family, and the love of Christ is healing his shattered heart. I'm specifically showing Lonnie who he is in Christ, and he is maturing as a believer. He feels a new power to love, and his wife has told me he's a new man under their old roof.

In this subject of choices, you can see that Lonnie made a conscious choice in this situation. He chose to forgive. He chose to be vulnerable and ask for help. As a result, the Lord is meeting his needs in ways Lonnie never believed were possible. He recently said to me, "I have learned that marriage is a holy trio with God at the center." I have seen him move from that "scared little boy" to becoming a decisive person who wants to live for the Lord and serve Him in his work, his home, and his church.

In counseling people like this, I have seen that much of our misery or blessing in life comes through our choices. Wrong choices eventually lead to dire consequences. Right choices lead to God's blessing in your life, even if that blessing brings with it other problems. Lonnie chose to let God's fruit come into his life by simply following God's principles for life. It's often a hard choice, but when thought through, when one seeks God, it's possible to turn a life around in radical ways.

CHOOSING OUR POWER SOURCE

In the previous chapter we looked at four choices we must make in the battle: (1) to seek and heed wise counsel; (2) to focus on other people; (3) to respond rightly to tough situations; and (4) to pray for God's help. There's a fifth choice we must make: to decide what power source we will rely on. Will we run on God's power—the Spirit of God filling and leading us—or will we seek other sources of power, such as drugs, alcohol, revenge, or hatred?

Choosing the right source of power is essential to spiritual peace and success. If our source is God, He offers many resources to empower us in the spiritual battle. Among them are knowing the Word of God, time in prayer, and the ability to have personal holiness. But if we cease to "plug in" to the right sources of power, the other elements of our relationship with God become murky.

The choice of the right power sources hit home to me in the case of Phil. As he stepped into my office, Phil looked like a whipped puppy. He sat down and exclaimed, "I feel that I have died spiritually. I can't pray and the Bible is as dry as sawdust. I need help."

His words seemed to echo those of Larry, whom we met in chapter 8. Larry's source of spiritual deadness was a lack of scriptural input in his life. The lack of spiritual power in Phil's life was much more than that. And as a Bible college graduate, he was both frustrated and puzzled.

His wife and he were rearing three wonderful children. But his job gave little joy. When I asked him about the workplace, his eyes turned dark and he scowled. "I hate my job," he replied, his voice dripping with bitterness. "The guys make fun of me because I am a believer."

We looked at several passages of Scripture that instruct us to rejoice in the midst of persecution. Somehow, though, I didn't sense this was really the problem. I encouraged Phil to be transparent with the Lord and open up with me.

Suddenly, Phil began to weep. A confession followed: "I gradually became complacent in my walk with the Lord. In time I quit reading the Bible and praying. I continued to attend church for my wife and children's sake. However, I began to look at some of the pornography that litters the walls of the office where I work. There is a young woman who works at the front desk. She began flirting with me. In time I started flirting back. One day I kissed her in the supply room and that's when I really became afraid of where I was going. The problem is, I don't know how to get back to where I belong with the Lord."

No Scripture. No prayer. Looking at lust-producing pictures. "Innocent" flirting and a stolen kiss. All those actions—and inactions— would push God's presence to the margins of Phil's life. We spent some time in prayer in which I asked the Lord to open Phil's heart and help him genuinely repent.

In a matter of minutes, Phil confessed the sins of breaking fellowship with the Lord, prayerlessness, and lack of Bible reading. He went on to ask the Lord to forgive him for looking at pornography and the lustful desires toward the young woman at work that quickly followed.

As we prayed and talked, I saw his face light up. Peace and joy from the Lord came into his heart and he exclaimed, "I'm free!"

Phil has changed vocations. Today he is the senior pastor of a growing church. He understands the wiles of the devil, and he has a great big heart full of love for struggling people. He tells his story to them as both an example of a prodigal son come back to his Father and a heavenly Father who welcomed him with an embrace and a party.

CHOOSING TO WHOM WE WILL SUBMIT

The sixth choice we must make is deciding to whom we will submit. When we not only submit to Christ's commands but make Him the leader of our lives, real intimacy with Christ develops. With this submission and intimacy come many resources for the battle: renewed faith, which dispels our fear; humility, which conquers our pride; self-sacrificing love, which overturns selfishness; and a greater willingness to please the Lord, which helps us overcome the power of the flesh.

When we choose not to submit, we are prone to several temptations, including an arrogant attitude, insisting on our rights to the harm of others, and uncontrolled anger. These all become spiritual battlegrounds. The choice to become angry—and it is a real choice; we are never "forced" to become angry—can lead to a life of horror.

Henry had this problem and came to me as a professing Christian. He said life was going well with one exception—his temper. As he talked, he told me about several times in recent weeks when he "lost it." One response startled me.

"I was driving on such-and-such a road when this jerk cut me off," Henry said, with a trace of irritation in his voice. "The jerk slowed down and refused to let me pass by keeping pace with a slow-moving vehicle in the left lane. We came to a stoplight several miles down the road. I jumped out of my car and beat on the side window of his car. I swore at him and challenged him to a fight. When he wouldn't look at me, I became even more angry." His voice rising, Henry added, "That stupid jerk was wrong to cause me to get mad."

At the end of his account, he paused. Then he asked, rather meekly, "Dr. Copley, what do you think?"

I'm always somewhat taken aback at what a person will do when angry, but I'm rarely shocked. I told him rather directly, "I think you have a problem controlling your anger. And if you don't get control of it, it will damage your life severely."

Henry gulped, but decided to listen to me as a counselor and someone who truly wanted to help him overcome this problem. Over the next four weeks, I told him more of what I thought, a little bit at a time—I didn't want him to get angry at me!

Such anger comes from many sources. Over time, I learned that Henry's father and grandfather also struggled with outbursts of anger. Henry learned it from these men and thought it was normal.

This, of course, reflects an unwillingness to submit to others. The thinking is, "I'm in charge; he can't do that to me!"

There's also frustration, attempting to control or regain control of a situation, lust, and the learned behavior of becoming angry whenever things don't go your way.

Although feeling angry is not a sin, continual anger leads to bitterness or rage, which are sins. Paul warned, "Be angry, and do not sin" (Ephesians 4:26). Rage is what some people do when they do not know what else to do. For many people, it's the first reaction they carry in their emotional pocketbook.

Regardless of the reasons for anger, though, the bottom line is that anger is a choice. In Henry's case, he chose to become angry. In fact, he lived on the edge of anger all the time, always ready to simply let it rip. In time Henry learned to cry out to God when situations came up that could lead to anger. To his delight he learned that one of the fruits of the Spirit is self-control (Galatians 5:23). As Henry learned to walk in the Spirit, he stopped giving in to the impulse to "cut loose."

To conquer the wrong choice of anger, one must make the right choice of meekness, or gentleness. This marks a submissive person. But what about when one becomes so angry he sins in out-of-control actions? What can fix such a situation? God's answer is for-giveness. To forgive requires humility, another mark of a submissive spirit. And when we forgive others who sin against us or hurt us, the Holy Spirit cuts out the diseased part of our hearts, the part that would react with anger. It's a kind of spiritual surgery, as if God Him-self had taken the knife and removed the offending organ.

Through counsel, reading the Scriptures, and memorizing and applying specific passages about anger, Henry has learned to submit to God: to obey Him and His directives. He has learned not to sub-mit to the emotion of the moment, the feeling of "righteous indig-nation" (it wasn't righteous, but he often thought it was), and the desire to get even.

It's all a matter of simple choice of whom you will submit to: God or the devil.

HUMILITY AND MEN

Submission means humility. And humility is the opposite of pride. The warning of Scripture is "God resists the proud, but gives grace to the humble" (James 4:6; see also Proverbs 3:34). A humble, sub-missive spirit seems a particular challenge for most men. The male ego does exist, and many men are driven by it.

I saw once again how this works in the case of Brent. "I've read warfare books, prayed steps to freedom, and I am trying to live the Christian life. What's wrong?" I sensed Brent's tremendous pride and knew what was at stake. We prayed together, and as I talked to the Lord, he said that the Spirit brought to his mind a "soul tie" he had with a married woman in his church. He had taken inappropriate sexual liberties with her. It did not lead to adultery, but he had truly "lusted after her in his heart," which Jesus called adultery in the Sermon on the Mount (see Matthew 5:27–28).

In my presence, Brent repented of this sin. I then turned him to the pride issue. Brent was an attractive man and was always flattered when women gave him attention. Moreover, his own wife would become jealous of the attention, and this in some way brought Brent even more pleasure.

I showed him through several Scriptures how this pride had hurt him and his marriage. Brent immediately confessed this entire sordid thing to the Lord as vain and asked for freedom from such pride. I watched as he humbled himself, even with tears. Today, he continues to confess the pride problem on nearly a daily basis. "The battle of self is not an easy one," he says, "for I have learned that I am my own worst enemy."

This had made Brent feel distant from God. He now sees what had happened. "The Bible says, 'the Lord resists the proud,' and I think God was resisting me," Brent says. "When the Lord resists us, we have no power to live the Christian life. That gave the enemy an opportunity to offer his substitutes: lust, pride, money, et cetera. Today I am thankful to be walking in fellowship with Jesus because He gives me all the grace I need to live for Him successfully."

Something else happened when Brent humbled himself. When he first visited me, his initial complaint was "There is something in my head telling me I will never be free; the voice keeps telling me it owns me." What happened to that voice assuring him he would never become free? It is gone. When truth showed up, it had no debating points left. It simply left the field.

How are your choices going this week? Spend some time each day talking to God about the choices you've made and the ones you have to make. He will give you insight and genuine help if you seek Him honestly.

CHAPTER THIRTEEN

FINAL CHOICES

The *R* word. Repentance is a concept with which even Christians at times struggle. It may be difficult for people to admit they're wrong, to agree with God that their attitudes and actions are sin. It's humbling to acknowledge to God—and often others—that your thoughts, words, or behaviors are wrong. Usually we must ask for forgiveness when we repent. And that's difficult, too.

But that's the next choice we must make: Will we choose repentance?

The enemy will do anything to keep us from this sacred reality. To repent means to "turn around, to change one's mind." Sometimes when we have sinned we do not recognize it; we do not acknowledge it. David realized this when he sinned with Bathsheba and wrote about his response to his adulterous act in Psalm 38:13: "But I, like a deaf man, do not hear; and I am like a mute who does not open his mouth."

David eventually was confronted with his sin of adultery and the subsequent murder of Bathsheba's husband—by a prophet, no less! (Read about it in 2 Samuel 12:1–9.) Like David, many of us have difficulty admitting we have sinned. We tend to deny, rationalize, or blame others for our sin/problems. We are like hypocrites who chant, "Faults in others I can see, but praise the Lord, there are none in me."

The truth is that only repentance brings hope. God actually has a solution to our sin problems. Through a simple act of repentance, we can be set free and set on a new course as if we were starting over! That doesn't mean there may not be consequences of our sin, but it does mean with God there is always a second chance, and a third one, and a hundredth one!

Our problem is when we sin we tend to justify ourselves. We choose to minimize the evil we have done. We may plead guilty, but always with a request to say something on our behalf. "Yes, but ..." and "I understand, but please let me say ... "

GENUINE REPENTANCE IS A CHOICE

But we must learn to accept responsibility for our actions, our misdeeds. A friend of mine found this out when he ran a stop sign. A policeman wrote him a ticket. He decided to go to court to defend himself. He told the judge that several cars ahead of him ran the stop sign before he did and they were not pulled over. He urged the judge, saying, "Your Honor, is it fair that they get off scot-free and I get the ticket?"

"Did you roll through the stop sign?" the judge asked.

"Yes, I did," my friend was forced to admit.

"Guilty," pronounced the judge. My friend paid the fine.

In the same way, as long as we justify our sin or blame others, we are listening to Satan's lies. We will only be free of sin when we see it as God sees it, when we recognize and turn from our misdeeds. How do we do this? We must come into His presence and there remain until all our self-serving arguments collapse and we fully repent. Then, and only then, do we come to that single mind, which is God's mind.

Ethel's sin was fear. Not fear of God, but fear of people and, to a lesser extent, fear of death. Those fears were prompted by an almost deadly encounter with a crime suspect. She called me one day from the psychological unit of the hospital. Her words came out slowly, deliberately, and full of pain as she related her story.

Ethel had joined the police force of a major city after graduating from the police academy, fulfilling her childhood dream of becoming a law enforcement officer. But in her third year as a policewoman, she was confronted with a gun at her head.

"My partner and I were called to a crime scene," Ethel told me. "The back door had been pried open. As I approached the door, a man leaped into the doorway with a drawn gun aimed at my head. He pulled the trigger on what was later identified as a .357 Magnum. The primer detonated but the gun did not fire. I fired before he had a second chance. He died in the hospital later that evening."

Ethel was alive, clearly by the grace of God, and I thought this should have made her very grateful toward God. It didn't. Instead, she said, "Since that day I have lost my confidence. I clutch in a crisis. Because of this I have made mistakes—enough to get fired from my job two days ago. Last night I took enough pills to, as my doctor says, kill a large horse; yet I lived. I see now that God has saved my life twice. But I'm confused. Please open your Bible and show me how I can have peace in my heart and become a whole person."

A PROPER FEAR OF GOD

The Lord led me to discuss "The fear of the Lord is the beginning of knowledge," from Proverbs 1, talking about how "fear" really means "reverence and trust."

Ethel soon admitted that even though she was a believer, she did not reverence or trust the Lord. From there, we talked about how the fear of other people can cause a Christian to stumble in his relationship with God. This made a lot of sense to her.

It was then I moved on to what the enemy was doing in her life. I explained that fear is a tormentor, and the enemy was using her twin crises—nearly being killed and taking a human life—to his own advantage. She nodded her head with understanding and said that for the first time in years, the need to trust God and not fear other people was real to her. Ethel recommitted her life to the Lord. I led her in prayer, and as we prayed, a window of understanding opened in her soul. She asked the Lord to take back the ground the enemy had taken in her soul.

In the weeks that followed, we studied the Scriptures together, and Ethel continued to confess sin as the Lord brought it to mind. Ethel began to grow spiritually, and her growth reminded me of a jack-in-the-box I had as a child. When the lid opened, Jack sprang out of the box. In Ethel's situation, when the sin was confessed and the lies were removed, she jumped out of Satan's box and the growth in her life was almost instantaneous.

Two years later Ethel said to me, "The Lord has put me in a desk job that I really enjoy. He has given me peace in my heart, and I now know I am a new creation in Christ. The fear is gone, and the Lord has replaced it with faith. That which Satan intended for evil the Lord is working for good."

When you trust God with everything in your life, you need fear no one on earth, in heaven, or anywhere else!

GROWING IN CHRIST IS A CHOICE

A key arena in which we have the power to make real choices is in growing spiritually. Spiritual growth follows repentance. The enemy will do his worst to keep us from getting saved, but if that happens, he changes his tactics. Now he will do everything to keep us from growing in Christ so that we can be effective in building His kingdom. He hates what the theologians call "progressive sanctification," and what the Scriptures tell us is becoming more like Christ as we seek to know Him more and, by the Spirit, sin less. See, for example, these Scriptures: John 17:17; 2 Corinthians 3:18; Romans 12:2; Ephesians 5:26; Philippians 1:6.

Elaine received Christ as Savior when she was sixteen; for the next two years, however, her spiritual growth was slow and sporadic. When she entered college she almost forgot she was a Christian. She earned her master's degree in education and landed the teaching position of her dreams. However, being an educator didn't bring the satisfaction she desired. She came to my office within weeks of being "dumped" by the man she was engaged to.

"I know I'm a Christian," Elaine stated in the first session, "but the Christian life doesn't work for me." She freely admitted that she did not read the Bible and rarely prayed. She also revealed that she struggled with bitterness toward her ex-fiancé and was addicted to cigarettes. As I shared principles of freedom with her, the Lord opened her eyes and heart. She repented of pride (running her own life) and bitterness. She sought the Lord's forgiveness for harming the Lord's temple through tobacco abuse. She asked the Lord to take back the ground she had given to the enemy.

Back home, she made Bible reading and prayer a daily part of her life. The Lord led her to a local church with a dynamic singles ministry.

"I have been walking with the Lord for three years," she later told me, "and He is changing my life. I am like an onion—He is peeling off the old life a layer at a time. But with each layer He removed, He's added to my life Christian virtues, increased godly desires, and greater knowledge of Himself. The Lord is doing what I am not capable of doing myself. He is causing me to grow into His likeness."

WE CHOOSE WHOM WE WILL LOVE

The final arena involves whom we will love. Spiritual growth leads to a level of life in Christ where we experience forgiveness, joy unspeakable, and the glory of God's presence. Loving Christ results in obedience, and obedience leads to worshiping God and loving others. We become peacemakers. We learn to endure in doing good. We stop "returning evil for evil" and, rather, we "return good for evil." The fruit of the Spirit characterize our lives. We begin choosing for God rather than against God.

Even as we choose to love, we recognize the unseen spiritual powers that oppose us (Ephesians 6:12). They will counsel us to lash out, hate, hold grudges, seek revenge, push people away, and do all kinds of nasty things that hurt relationships. When we recognize that such thinking is the essence of spiritual warfare, we can begin to deal with it in the Lord's power. We also will find comfort, even healing, in our lives.

The choice to love proved to be healing and transforming in Andy's life. He looked angry enough to spit bullets. As he told his story, I could understand his frustration. An injustice had occurred against his son, and it included verbal and physical abuse. But Andy's response was also excessive. He was full of anger, perhaps even hate. Rather than love and forgive, Andy sounded like he was ready to level the offender.

"Last Sunday afternoon at church, while my wife was at a ladies' function, this idiot was watching the kids while they played in the gym. My son stepped outside the door to get a drink of water. My boy was unaware that he needed permission to get a drink of water.

"Then this guy in charge grabbed him by the arm, dragged him back into the gym, and threw him down the bleachers. He then proceeded to give my son a tongue-lashing in front of the other children and refused to let him get up for the next two hours. The guy even refused him permission to use the bathroom.

"I called him on this after the next service. This man then blasted me about what a creep my son was.

"Last week four other people who had the same problem with the man—a true idiot—called to offer their sympathy. The grapevine works quite well at our church. I really want a piece of this guy. What should I do?"

I don't normally give out advice on how to take people down, so I quickly decided to move the conversation in a new direction. I told him I have experienced similar problems over the years, so I could in part identify with how he was feeling. It was then I brought up the subject of forgiveness. I explained how Andy's bitterness was not only obnoxious but hurting him. Given time, it would "defile" or "stain" others around him (see Hebrews 12:15).

Andy trembled a bit. I wondered if he actually sensed the serious nature of his bitterness or if he wanted a "piece of me." But he nodded agreement; he became calm. Then the Lord granted him grace to forgive. The bitterness was swept out of his heart and it was replaced with the love of God. His twelve-year-old son found it quite easy to forgive the same man.

Four years later, Andy wrote and explained what he did after he left the office.

Dr. Copley,
I began praying for the man that I was previously bitter towards. The Lord prompted me to pray that he would develop a love for children. Last Wednesday evening the same man gave a testimony in prayer meeting. He told how the Lord had given him a deep love for children. That love became so strong that he and his wife chose to have a child of their own. He went on to tell about the blessings his little son had become to him. He is truly a changed man, and so am I. I am learning that the very thing God wanted to use to bless and strengthen me—my son—the devil tried to use to make me bitter.

Andy had learned that the grace of God is greater than any sin.

I believe the thing that is killing many believers' testimonies today is bitterness. When a believer is bitter, his attitude has the effect of saying to the enemy, "I have opened the door of my life to you, so come and influence me."

The Lord's answer to bitterness is always forgiveness. This is a signpost of love. Forgiving others when they despise us (or despise those we love) is supernatural. And it comes from having an *agape* love that will love others no matter what.

Ultimately, giving love—and forgiveness—is a real choice each of us must make nearly every day.

BEYOND THE DECEPTIONS

PART FOUR

1. Has someone offended you? How will you deal with him?

2. When the Holy Spirit reveals sin in your life, what will you choose to do?

WE HAVE
THE CHURCH

THE GREAT DECEPTION... AND THE TRUTH

SATAN'S LIE: "Abandon the church. It is no longer relevant; it is old-fashioned." (See Hebrews 10:25.)

GOD'S TRUTH: *"The church of the living God [is] the pillar and ground of the truth"* (1 Timothy 3:15).

CHAPTER FOURTEEN

THE CHURCH
AS A
PRIMARY
RESOURCE

The armor of God. The Holy Spirit. The truth of God's Word. Holy living. We have seen many resources for fighting Satan's lies thrown at us during the spiritual battle. But one of the enemy's greatest lies is directed at one of God's greatest resources—the local church. The lie is: "Abandon the church. It's old-fashioned; you can serve God well enough without it." The truth is: The church is "the pillar and ground of the truth" (1 Timothy 3:15).

The apostle Paul was direct: "The church of the living God [is] the pillar . . . of the truth." That means it is God's appointed institution to execute His program of witness, service, and building up of the saints. Jesus Himself said, "I will build My church, and the gates of Hades shall not prevail against it" (Matthew 16:18). The universal church, as expressed through the local church, serves as the primary bastion of defense and offense against the enemy in the world today. Winning souls, revival, spiritual warfare, discipleship, discipline, corporate prayer, and missionary endeavors are carried out under the leadership of the local assembly. The church brings converts into the church for nurture, growth, and instruction that includes training for the battle against evil forces. In that sense, the local church becomes the base of operations for these converts to invade Satan's kingdom and win souls to Christ.

Because of this, Satan does attack the church, both its leaders and its membership. The warfare can be disheartening at times and seemingly brutal. Church splits do happen. But God will protect His chosen institution, and often He does intercede in broken churches, particularly when His people pray. Young pastor Charlie Smith (not his real name) found that out at his very first church.

Fresh out of seminary, Charlie couldn't wait to move to the parsonage of the church that had just called him as senior pastor. Armed with a master's degree and full of zeal, Charlie planned to set the world on fire. His face glowed as he thought of preaching in the pulpit of this beautiful auditorium that still smelled new. The unanimous vote boosted his spirits, and he looked forward to leading a unified church.

Within days of unloading the moving van and helping his wife and two young children settle in, Charlie realized the unanimous vote actually came from two factions that had split months before but were unwilling to leave the new building. Each side claimed a right to own it and remain, with the other group leaving. Each group also believed Charlie was their man.

SPIRITUAL WARFARE IN THE CHURCH

Several days after getting started, Charlie learned the chairman of the elder board was involved in an affair with a young married woman who was also a member of the church. The former pastor would not confront the issue; instead he chose to answer a call to greener and calmer pastures. During his early sermons Charlie saw a smirk on the face of the head elder almost as often as he observed the closed eyes of the elder who dozed through every sermon. Charlie began to dream of the "good old seminary days," when he carried a full course load and also worked forty hours a week in the freezer at the meat packing plant to make ends meet. That was difficult, but it didn't compare to the stress of this pastorate.

Each group pulled on Charlie as members jockeyed for position to take over the facility. Nearly every church event turned into a power play. Even a solemn event like a funeral became a show of force. One faction would tell Charlie, "You better not give him a Christian funeral. If anybody ever went to hell, he did." His sin? Siding with the other faction, of course.

The only warfare instruction Charlie had ever received in seminary was some teaching on the theological liberalism that had invaded the church. Excellent teaching that this was, Charlie was ill prepared for the all-out internal warfare going on in his pews. Though he also studied about church conflicts and how to "be in charge of the war" in a church situation, nothing in his class notes shed light on the present problem. Without a question the enemy was behind this assault on the church, using all his classic tactics to divide and conquer.

During this time, Charlie began to wonder if the enemy's purpose was not only to destroy the ministry of the church but to seriously blemish the reputation of the Lord. This hurt even more than the idea that the church itself might go down.

So Charlie began to pray. He realized God had ordained the church for His service, and he asked the Lord to oppose whatever forces were at work in the church. He actually pleaded with God for a miracle.

As he sought the Lord, the Spirit brought to Charlie's attention a group of committed saints who took neither side. He discovered that they, often with tears, were praying desperately for the church in the way only scared but committed saints can do: with passion, love, and genuine hope that God would answer.

The group prayed, and Charlie led them with the hope of "winning one for the Father."

One night a verse jumped off the page of the Bible as Charlie read, "The time has come for judgment to begin at the house of God" (1 Peter 4:17). Not sure what this meant, Charlie prayed that this would indeed be God's operative plan. However, he didn't really expect what was about to happen.

THE JUDGMENT OF GOD

The next day the leader of one of the factions died quite suddenly. It did cross Charlie's mind that God might have "struck him down," even as He had struck Ananias, Sapphira, and Herod Antipas (see Acts 5:1–11; 12:20–23). Pastor Charlie didn't say anything about his thoughts as he preached this leader's funeral; he did not try to rally anyone against the other group nor even mention the conflict. But as he preached, the other leader suddenly fell sick, went into the hospital, and was not expected to live. Charlie visited him and prayed for him. By the unique grace of God, this second leader did live, and then accepted Christ while he was in the hospital.

God, who had interceded twice already, was ready to act through this new child of His. One morning three weeks later, the converted elder stood before the congregation, gave his testimony, and then pleaded for forgiveness. As if setting in motion the gears of a great machine that had been idle, a genuine revival broke out. People crossed the aisles to seek forgiveness from one another. The chairman of the elders was disciplined for his adultery. Within a few short years, the church, now committed to honoring God, doubled in size. Charlie watched it all unfold, as astonished as the rest, but grateful that God had known what to do about the problem even if he hadn't.

Through that experience, Charlie grew in his understanding of spiritual warfare as he searched and taught the Scriptures in order to build up the flock. He also warned the flock over and over that the wolf remained ready to attack again, so they must be vigilant and ready, as Paul said to the Ephesians in Acts 20:28–30. Charlie saw clearly there are two kingdoms operating in God's world, and they are mutually exclusive. He also learned that Jesus is the ultimate Lord of both kingdoms.

NOT UNIQUE

This example, while a bit unusual, is not unique. God loves His church and protects it. In chapter 15 we will see how Satan can infect a church, but we need to know how God defends and uses the church mightily in spiritual battles.

Again, the local church serves as the primary fortress and offense against the enemy. If you are a Christian and are not involved in a church, it's my hope that chapters 14–16 will not only convince you of the church's position before God and its power, but also of your own need to become allied with other Christians in the struggle.

Lone Rangers rarely last long in the church. That's why it's called "the body of Christ." In that sense, Jesus Himself needs us to accomplish His purpose as much as we need Him. The miracle of Christianity is that God has made us His coworkers. Not slaves, nor merely servants. But coworkers and those who will share in the harvest!

THE POWER OF THE CHURCH

What power does the church possess under God's authority in spiritual warfare? What can we, as members of the local church, expect to see happen when God is truly ruling there?

The power of the church is the power of every single Christian: the Holy Spirit. But in the church that power is enlarged through unified believers. Remember, before the disciples received the Holy Spirit they were in a sense powerless, the same way any unbeliever is today. However, afterward, they experienced incredible power as together they began to impact their society. In the book of Acts we see three amazing results occurred when the Holy Spirit came upon the church:

- The church experienced growth in numbers (Acts 2:5–41).
- The church experienced growth spiritually (Acts 10:47–48; 15:32; 19:17–20). Spiritual growth typically results in numerical growth. Healthy Christians reproduce themselves.
- The church experienced persecution from her enemies (Acts 5:17–42; 14:3–7).

I'm not saying these are things that will always happen to any church where the Spirit is working. Sometimes, depending on the situation and for other reasons, a church does not grow dramatically or even incrementally even though there seems to be real spiritual growth.

Keep in mind, however, that any church where Christians develop genuine maturity and/or numerical prosperity is subject to spiritual assault by the great deceiver. In fact, I believe the enemy will certainly launch a counterattack. He recognizes that Christ's kingdom is the ardent enemy of the kingdom of darkness. When Satan sees his own strongholds tumbling down, he must act. Often this comes in the form of persecution. It's then that the power of the Spirit is so crucial.

Charlie himself saw God's direct power levied on his congregation as a result of prayer and commitment. This power rarely happens in one person alone. Generally, God uses it in the many, uniting them together in a cause that is greater than any single person's vision.

THE POWER OF A CHURCH'S VISION

Such unity comes when the people have a common vision. I was reminded of this years ago when I directed a discussion with the pastors and elders of a church in the Midwest during a two-day retreat. The church was being pulled in several directions. As I spent time with the church leaders before the retreat, five areas of conflict came to the forefront. There were relational, spiritual, doctrinal, philosophical, and organizational conflicts among the people of the congregation.

As each problem was brought up, the forty-plus of us would gather together and ask the Spirit of God to guide us. What soon became evident was the lack of a clear vision statement for the body. When I would ask individuals what their vision was for this body of Christ, they had no answer. I advised them to seek God and His vision of what He wanted to do in their midst.

During the actual retreat, we hammered out a vision statement that everyone agreed upon. The mission statement went like this: "This local church exists for the purpose of loving Jesus Christ by magnifying Him through the Word and worship, by loving believers and encouraging them toward maturity and ministry, and by loving the lost through making Jesus Christ known to our neighbors and the world."

This mission statement gave the leaders of the church a purpose and a direction. They next evaluated the programs of their church. In the process, some of them were discarded because they did not fit into the mission statement of the church. Others were added.

As the leaders moved forward in the process, their hearts were unified. It was not uncommon during that weekend to see them break down in tears of repentance and forgiveness toward each other. The power of their vision made possible not only direction and unity but also greater love and commitment toward each other.

God wants us to have His vision. As a congregation walks with the Lord, the members are to walk in the unity of the Spirit, which He has established in His body. Now, several years later, the church is strong, it has grown, there is solid unity among the people, and God is being glorified.

THE NEED TO STAND FIRM AND RESIST

What then is the church to do when persecution results? The church is to *stand firm against the enemies of our Lord, whether these enemies are human or demonic.* This is what Charlie discovered was his main mission: not to attack; not to tear down; not to fear or cower; but to stand firm, to hold the ground he had, and to let God lead this group into ever-widening territory.

In light of this, churches are to be wary, vigilant, and refuse to give in to the tactics of the enemy. That calls for standing on the foundation of the Word. It's like a sumo wrestler taking up his position on a mat; the church and its leaders retain their balance, ready to resist a shove or pull from any direction. Satan will try to knock the church and its members off balance, but if they are strong in the Word and ready for such an assault, they will not easily be moved, let alone knocked down. Unlike the sumo wrestler, we have much more than a skimpy loincloth; we have the complete armor of God at our disposal.

A friend of mine I'll call Austin pastors a progressive church in a fairly large city. After he began his ministry there, he learned two factions had kept the church divided for ten years. Both of these factions had different ideas on what the church was to do. He called me one day and asked if I would be willing to help his people come to a new vision for the church. Austin wanted me to give an outside perspective and help unify the two split factions within his church.

The leaders and I met in a pleasant country setting, about an hour's drive away from the church. We spent the first hour in prayer and worship. Then, as we rose from our time of worship, I asked each of the church leaders and their wives to share their burden for the church. I jotted notes as they spoke.

Amazingly, I kept hearing the same thing, which is unusual when you have factions like this. Of course, it was all phrased in different words and different ways, but it was basically the same thing. They wanted to glorify God and to do His will through the body.

When this clarified, we capitalized on how we could glorify God and make ourselves available as vessels to function in His body. We turned to problems that might hinder the body, and we soon found that there were several leaders with an extremely critical spirit. As we confronted that as a body, the Lord brought conviction and repentance to these members.

At that point, we moved on to the vision the Lord wanted to give these leaders. Several Scriptures helped the leaders' thinking: "Lift up your eyes and look at the fields, for they are already white for harvest" (John 4:35), "Whatever you do, do all to the glory of God" (1 Corinthians 10:31), and "Bear one another's burdens"(Galatians 6:2). Before the weekend retreat was finished, it appeared everyone had moved toward the mind of Christ—one mind leading the entire body. The folks understood they might see things differently from others, but that was only because each had different gifts that guided their hopes and desires. Now seeing this for what it was, they realized their factionalism had been a lie of Satan. In reality, they were much more unified than they originally thought. And there was a brand-new commitment to serving together for the glory of God.

Recently I was able to talk to Austin about the results of this meeting; he described a new enthusiasm—an enthusiasm the church had never experienced in the previous ten years. Now their Sunday evening gatherings begin with prayer, which usually lasts an hour or more before they actually get to the preaching. They're bringing more diversified people into the body. A new love for each other permeates the body. And there is fresh understanding of the work of the enemy.

"Understanding the lies of the enemy and understanding the mind of Christ has brought new life into the church," Austin concludes.

STANDING FIRM AGAINST SATAN'S LIES

Satan's lies against the church are often subtle. But they can also be direct, as can his actions. He can use people to influence members' lives. Let me tell you about Pastor Sam. As his suburban church thrived and honored God, he felt his ministry could hardly get any better. Hundreds of people found Christ through the ministry of this New York church. Pastor Sam found church growth to be one of the most exhilarating things he had ever experienced. A seminary even gave Sam an honorary doctor of divinity degree in recognition of his excellent work. Preaching to hundreds of people weekly fulfilled his life dream.

Sam did not take into account that the enemy might want to undermine this great work. He didn't reckon with the fact that great victory invites great danger. Perhaps spiritual pride had set in. While a believer is occupied with the blessings of God, the devil schemes to steal it all away.

Satan's scheme in Sam's church was to appear as an "angel of light." A well-groomed lady with position, power, and money joined the church. This "sister," whom we'll call Angeline, quickly won the hearts of the church leaders through her charm, physical presence, and downright "spiritual" ability. In a short time Angeline was given a major position of leadership. She befriended and visited every family in the church. She spent thousands of dollars of her own money on new equipment for the ministry. Over the next two years, she became deeply enmeshed into church life. A willing worker, a "humble" friend, she seemed to be sent from heaven. This all changed abruptly.

Early one Monday morning, Pastor Sam went by the church to retrieve something he left the evening before. When he walked into the building, he received the shock of his life. This woman had stayed in the building Sunday night. During the night she had erected an altar behind the pulpit. On the altar lay the pictures of most of the families in the church. Candles were burning and Sam soon realized some sort of ceremony was taking place. In time, he was to find out this was actually a satanic ritual meant to claim every soul in his church.

Shortly after Pastor Sam walked in on her, a male voice spoke through Angeline. The voice told the pastor there was a church of several thousand members in the area, and the voice said it knew the exact date the pastor would resign. It promised him the pulpit as the next senior pastor if he would cooperate with the voice.

Sam ignored the voice. He turned, went to his office, and called the police. They removed the woman, and the items on the altar were burned.

Sam thought this was the end, but mass confusion gripped his people. Sam invited me to help stabilize the situation. This woman, who had appeared to be so spiritual and committed, was actually an emissary of Satan. Sam told me Angeline was later identified as part of a satanic cult operating in the area.

I knew it would be difficult, but Sam believed God was in the situation (as He always is), and for three weeks I counseled individual families ten hours a day and preached each evening. The revelation of candles burning before members' pictures sent fear through the congregation. During this time I met with every family in the church, discovering problems and sins that had "spun out of control" during the time of this woman's tenure. We prayed for the Lord's wisdom and searched the Scriptures for His answers.

For instance, one family I'll call the Dakins had turned to alcohol during this very difficult time in the church. It started with Angeline bringing the family a bottle of wine when she came to visit. She would quote the Scriptures where Paul told Timothy to take a little wine for his infirmities. However, it seemed as if Angeline had some sort of unique insight into this family situation, for before the husband and wife became Christians they both had been alcoholics. During this time of mass confusion they went back to comforting themselves with alcohol rather than the Word and people of God. By the time I was able to spend an afternoon with the Dakins, they were addicted to alcohol again and it was on the verge of spinning out of control. I believe this woman purposely set up the Dakins to bring destruction in their lives.

Thankfully, God was able to work through that, and as I talked with the husband and wife, they both repented of the sin with many tears and asked God to redeem the situation. Later that day Mr. and Mrs. Dakin asked their children's forgiveness for the example they had set and how they had sinned before them. Still later yet they expressed repentance to the entire church. What was the enemy's lie here? "Yes, you were once addicted, but now that you are Christians you are stronger. This may even be scriptural."

Over that time, the Lord graciously gave light and understanding and soon restored the church. At the same time, Pastor Sam's eyes opened to the reality of warfare: Satan walks around roaring like a lion seeking whom he may devour.

The church lost several families. Some could not believe Angeline could do such things, and felt the church had misunderstood her and overreacted. One family chose to believe Angeline's accusation against the church leaders, despite her Sunday night burning in the church. Three other families said, in essence, "If the leadership has no more discernment than this, we don't feel protected here." And thus they went elsewhere. Angeline had sown her wicked seeds. But the church recovered; indeed it is a growing church, one where the Lord is being honored. But the question remains: How did this woman gain such power in the church?

The truth is, there are many people like this. Few worship Satan, but they are under his influence and open to suggestions. They may not even realize they are simply pawns of the devil. But they invade and then infect the church with the kind of turmoil that can split it, lead people into sin, or provoke doctrinal shifts that render the church unusable by God.

No church is immune from the implant of a satanic infiltrator. Again, they may not be a part of an organized cult or satanic group. Disgruntled "Christians" coming from another church may serve the enemy just as skillfully; so can long-term members who disagree with one another and begin to choose sides (the situation at Charlie's church).

HOW SHOULD THE CHURCH RESPOND?

How should the church deal with these people—those from within and without the church who can be used by the enemy? The following principles are of utmost importance while ministering to such people:

First, prayer is our ultimate weapon. Thus we must "pray without ceasing." Second, we must love the individuals whom the enemy is attempting to work through. We must build a relationship with them (they are often extremely needy). Remember God promises to be there with us (Matthew 18:20). Third, we must gain some insight about the type of occult or satanic involvement any individual may have willingly or often unwillingly participated in.

Those who are attacking leaders, spreading heresy, or dividing the church should be confronted with their actions and God's truth, according to the model of Matthew 18:15–17. Some will not respond to God's truth and will need to be removed (Titus 3:10). Others will respond to Christ's love and become new creations in Him. Keep your options open to the leading of the Holy Spirit. Other responses and specific stratagems will be presented in chapters 15–16.

HOW GOD CAN BREAK THROUGH

During a spiritual warfare conference years ago, I sat at a table with a friend of mine when a young lady, probably in her midthirties, walked over and took a seat beside us. As we were waiting to be served the evening meal, I struck up a conversation with her. To my absolute shock she knew far more than I did on the subject of spiritual warfare. As we continued to talk, I found that she was single, a registered nurse, and a member of a church whose pastor I knew very well. I listened to her talk about warfare. She had gone places I had never been. Finally she looked at me and said, "You are curious as to who I am, aren't you?"

I said, "Ma'am, I cannot understand how you can have the level of knowledge and insight you have, considering your age and occupation."

At that point she shared a story. "I was a witch in a coven. I was sent as a plant to such-and-such church to destroy it. I went in and did what I was assigned to do. I began to build relationships and curse various people, such as the pastor, but in time as he preached the gospel of Jesus Christ, his message began to reach my heart. One day God opened my spiritual eyes and I trusted Christ as my Savior."

I sat there amazed, my throat tight.

She went on. "Now I am born again and a growing Christian. God has brought me freedom in Christ. I have renounced everything in my past. I have an intense hunger for God and His Word. The Lord is using me to win others to Jesus Christ. He is using me in the counseling ministry to help others come to the freedom that only can be found in Him. I rejoice that God saved me, because I know if I had remained a witch I would have ended up in hell."

Sometime later I had an opportunity to share with the pastor of her church how exciting it was to meet this young woman. He smiled and said, "You don't know the half of it."

He then told me what he had seen with this lovely lady. When she initially arrived at his church, he had a feeling she had come from the local coven. His church is an aggressive body that does tremendous damage to the gates of hell, and that was why the coven was eager to destroy it. He said, "I immediately alerted the leaders of the church to pray for her. They were very careful to hold her before the throne of grace daily, and not to bring accusations against her or even tell her of our suspicions. As we gently reasoned with her and prayed for her, God broke through the thick layer of lies and years of pain, and the Word of God penetrated her heart and God gave her new life."

I agreed this had to be a special case, and he said, "Sometimes churches are too quick to remove someone who does not fit in with them. God may in His sovereignty be bringing that person into that body to come to Jesus Christ."

It's a tough call. But Christians walking with Christ and a church united in spirit need fear no one.

CHAPTER FIFTEEN

WHEN YOUR
CHURCH
BECOMES
INFECTED

The great deceiver uses his many tricks in many churches. Because believers comprise the local church and the enemy has the ability to deceive believers (see 2 Corinthians 11:3; 2 Timothy 2:25; 1 Thessalonians 3:5), we should not be surprised at his successes.

In fact, Satan was tempting and creating havoc within the earliest New Testament churches. Paul issued warnings about the tempter to the churches in Corinth and Thessalonica, and he warned the young yet God-fearing Timothy and other godly servants not to quarrel but to be kind and gentle to everyone (see Ephesians 4:31–32; 2 Timothy 2:24).

All of us become duped at one time or another, no matter how careful we are. We are most open to deceit, though, when we are not connected with the Lord through the Scriptures, prayer, and obedient living. People seek the wrong things in the church and turn to other resources, such as the occult, in order to get them.

WATCH OUT FOR
COUNTERFEIT TRUTH

Satan is in the business of destroying churches. What then are his greatest weapons in destroying them? Let me give you four primary methods he uses to undermine leadership and stop a church's progress.

First, Satan can counterfeit the truth. We have seen this in the previous chapter. Consider the elder board chairman at Charlie's church who became involved with a young married woman in the church. That elder rejected God's truth about adultery's sin and consequences and accepted Satan's supposed truths. Though we do not know which counterfeit truths the church elder accepted, Satan offers several counterfeits: "It's only a harmless, temporary fling; it could energize your marriage." "Look out for yourself. You have needs, after all, and surely God understands those needs have to be met." "God will forgive your indiscretions later. You can confess and agree with Him." There are many other counterfeit truths Satan feeds adulterers.

Meanwhile, in the suburban New York church where Angeline did the devil's work, one couple accepted as truth Angeline's accusation against the church leaders, despite her satanic ritual in the church. Others felt Angeline had been misunderstood in her actions. They concluded the church leaders had overreacted.

WATCH OUT FOR
COUNTERFEIT SPIRITUAL FRUIT

Second, Satan can give great feelings, and believers, remembering feelings of joy, even ecstasy, upon their conversion and first weeks with the Lord, may associate good feelings with spirituality. Some Christians crave those joyful feelings they experienced at the end of a weekend retreat—the so-called "mountaintop high"—as proof all is right between God and them. With great feelings, these believers think they must be "spiritual" because they "feel so good."

But feelings are fleeting and dangerous. Extreme emotional highs often produce extreme emotional lows.

Yes, the fruit of the spirit includes joy (and peace, for that matter), but we should not test our spirituality by seeing if strong emotions are constantly present. Where fruit is present on an ongoing basis, we can be more assured we are walking in the Spirit. Patience, kindness, goodness, self-control, and the other fruit listed in Galatians 5:22–23 should be evident in a believer's life.

Courtney loved those moments of high emotion, and Satan seemed to use them to delude her about her relationship with God. As we visited together in a counseling session, Courtney said, "I think I am a religious-high junkie." She explained that over the past few years when any big-name faith healer visited the area she would go to the services. Sometimes she gave large amounts of money against her husband's wishes. Several of those times she was able to talk to the faith healer, and he or she would lay hands on Courtney and offer some type of "imparted wisdom" to her. She told me, "Dr. Copley, the feeling was absolute ecstasy. The exhilaration was like nothing I had ever experienced."

I could imagine that it was! She went on. "But there was one problem. It would never last. I would always have to seek another high. Besides that, the lows became extremely low."

As we talked about the Christian life, I was able to show her that the normal Christian life is one in which we walk in love with Jesus Christ, and go where He leads us by His Spirit and through His Word. I told her that while there might be times of ecstasy and exhilaration, these experiences were always preceded by a reason. "For instance," I said, "King David danced before the ark when it was returned by the Philistines. He experienced ecstasy and worship. But he had a strong reason to do so—the glory of God."

She agreed, and I added, "As we walk with the Lord in a personal love relationship with Him led by His Spirit through the Scriptures, we can live a life that glorifies God without any counterfeit joy or peace or exhilaration that might not be from Him in reality."

Courtney began seeking God through the Scriptures and prayer and found through the practice of true Christian disciplines her life evened out and became much more stable.

WATCH OUT FOR
COUNTERFEIT HEALING

Satan can also counterfeit healing (see 2 Thessalonians 2:9). You can be sure the enemy will seek to counterfeit anything that is truly from God, even healing. I believe God can and on occasion does heal in the day in which we live. To say that He does not is to deny the power of God. Many times, though, He does not choose to heal. I have seen situations where people have sought out certain ailing Christians to persuade them to receive the healing that they so desperately needed.

Shawn was so duped. He had been diagnosed with schizophrenia in his early twenties. He had battled this debilitating illness for several years by taking antipsychotic medications. Because of modern scientific research, we have found that many drugs can take such people from a highly dysfunctional condition to a rather "normal" state of mind. In Shawn's case, he found that when he would take his drugs properly he could work a job, think with clarity, and function well. However, he always felt somewhat dull and "stupefied," which is a typical side effect of such drugs.

Shawn came to my office after being released from the psychiatric ward in the local hospital. He told me right away, "Dr. Copley, some weeks ago a faith healer came to town and I went forward. The faith healer laid hands on me and then he pronounced me healed of my schizophrenia. The strangest thing was I had not told him I was schizophrenic. After he laid hands on me I felt like a lightning bolt suddenly charged through my body. I walked out of that place feeling higher than I ever have in my life. As a result, I stopped taking my medication cold turkey."

Listening, I realized he was in much distress about this. He went on. "For the next fifteen days I was higher than a kite. I was happy, bubbly, personable, striking up conversations with strangers, full of energy, shouting out loud hallelujahs, and it was great. But then I bottomed out, and I ended up back in the hospital, back on my medications, back to living life as I had. What happened to me?"

I said, "What happened to you was you became the victim of a false healing. That which God truly does He does permanently. We have an enemy, and the enemy wants to deceive and disillusion us and eventually destroy us through these deceptions. One of those is false healing. I'm sorry to say. God probably wants you to take your medication, perhaps for the rest of your life."

Shawn agreed and has been normal ever since. But he was actually lucky. I have heard of good Christian people like him who have committed suicide or slipped into deeper psychosis as a result of such deceptions. I believe it's possible for God to heal completely in such cases. But it's rare. The more common way God "heals" is through modern medical techniques, which are legitimate and can help people immensely.

Keep in mind that Satan does empower for false healings, partial healings, and even occasional full healings to lead people away from God.

WATCH OUT FOR COUNTERFEIT POWER

Finally, Satan can grant limited power. Many people seek power or control—sometimes both. Satan, who has temporary rule over this world, has power that he can bestow. It is limited compared to that of God almighty, but it is still power, and this counterfeit power can woo and impress and deceive us.

It's easy to understand why power is so appealing. We all have a sense of personal inadequacy. There are times in counseling that the client and I both reach a state of hopeless despair at our own inadequacy to solve a problem. It's at that point that we cry out to God for His help, because when we are weak, God is strong (see 2 Corinthians 12:9–10). There's nothing wrong with this, and it's certainly not that bad a place to be. When we realize the need for help beyond what this world has to offer, we are being exactly what God made us all along: dependent creatures who need His love and power to survive.

Many people, though, seek the wrong kind of power: the power of Satan. And Satan does have earthly power; that's why he could offer Jesus the kingdoms of this world (see Matthew 4:8–9). Today Satan offers different kinds of power to Christ's followers. Some of the power sources that come from the enemy are:

- Signs and miracles.
- False ecstatic worship, which is actually a highly toxic mysticism. The fruit from this worship is weak, which in turn produces weak Christians.
- The false promise of health and wealth if you love God and have faith.
- False authority. Those who have such authority refuse to be tested in their faith by mature brothers.

I see this all the time among church members and even pastors. Hans, age twenty-eight, was a Bible college graduate and for two years the pastor of a small church in a medium-size city. But despite his pastoral credentials, he looked worn and weary when he entered my office. His shoulders drooped, his forehead was wrinkled, and his eyes were bloodshot.

He soon explained the cause of his weariness. "At first things were OK as pastoring goes," Hans said. "In time, though, I grew so weary of the people who continued to complain and of those who did not want to grow as Christians. Some days I felt overrun by the lack of nursery workers and Sunday school teachers. There never were enough. And one workday at the church, my wife and I were the only two who showed up."

A HUNGER FOR "SOMETHING ELSE"

Hans began to hunger for something else. As he read the Scriptures, he began to wonder if the apostolic gifts were still in place. This became an obsession with him. This gave the enemy an opportunity to introduce him to "Apostle Smith," who referred to himself as "the apostle." Apostle Smith quickly befriended Hans; he became the father Hans had never had growing up. Hans felt he had reason to trust Apostle Smith. He held Ph.D. and Th.D. degrees from respected schools. He had authored three books, which read well, and he had a warm, sincere charm about him. Finally, Apostle Smith had more than thirty churches under his authority—most of them planted under Smith's direction. Each of these churches gave a portion of their income to the apostle.

Hans should have thought about it when the apostle came to town in a stretch limo. However, he was too enamored of the apostle to consider it, something that typically happens with average pastors who meet so-called successful people in the ministry.

What really hooked Hans was when Apostle Smith showed personal interest in him. Apostle Smith seemed to really care about his struggles in the ministry and seemed to be eager to help in any way he could. Apostle Smith also seemed to have some unique powers. He could touch someone on the forehead and they would fall backward and be out like a light. He also seemed to have the gift of healing. He said several of his former parishioners claimed to be healed when Apostle Smith laid hands on them. Apostle Smith taught that all New Testament gifts were to be operating in the church, including tongues, miracles, healings, and raising of the dead.

After some time and many in-depth conversations, the apostle said, "Hans, your church is in trouble." Hans agreed. "It would be much wiser," the apostle continued, "if you took a group from your church and started a new work where you are going to truly restore the apostolic power that God wants in the church today." He explained that only God's "new wine" would be used in the restoration of true apostolic authority; Hans would know who was "new wine."

Hans was eager and more than willing to follow the Apostle's counsel, so he made an announcement and terminated his pastorate. He went down the street, rented a building, and one-third of the church followed him. The Apostle helped organize the new church. Then he ordained Hans into the new denomination—which claimed to be nondenominational—that had just about everything it needed except the power of God.

Whatever the source of his powers, Apostle Smith offered theological and doctrinal error. Significantly, he multiplied his "ministry" by splitting churches. Multiplication by division is a faulty formula. The apostle Paul wrote, "Reject a divisive man after the first and second admonition, knowing that such a person is warped and sinning, being self-condemned" (Titus 3:10–11). Apostle Smith was a divisive man.

The apostle was in charge of churches in five different states located in the South and Midwest. Among his false teachings was that he followed in the apostolic succession of the apostle Paul, who (he said) had oversight of the churches. Apostle Smith claimed to simply be one of many apostles the Lord had raised up worldwide to restore true power to the church in the "last days." The leadership of several charismatic denominations had condemned his practices and some of his teachings. In one state, a Pentecostal denomination wrote to its churches warning them of his unethical practices.

Unfortunately Hans was unaware of this at the time. Both the power and personal dynamics of the apostle swayed the pastor. "Apostle Smith is an excellent preacher," Hans told me. "People sit spellbound as they listen to him tell of people who have been healed and the dead who have been raised through his ministry."

During the next fourteen months, Hans saw his life fall apart. When the apostle saw that Hans's health was in decline, he strongly urged Hans to resign. He would replace Hans with a man who was personally trained by the apostle himself. Hans was out of a job and had no way to get another one.

Now, several years later, after much counseling and personal turmoil, Hans looks back and says, "I was deceived. A man came along and offered false authority with a false gospel. Because I was not connected to the Lord and clinging to Him by walking in the Word of God, I was a ripe target for Satan."

God has restored Hans; he is walking in truth, he loves Jesus Christ, and he is serving the Lord in another denomination in a way that brings great glory to God. And he doesn't want to hear from anyone who calls himself an "apostle" who moves from town to town in a stretch limo![1]

It's up to the church to expose Satan's counterfeit power with God's truth. When the church operates in the power of the Holy Spirit, the result will be seen in true conversions, changed lives, genuine love, and world evangelism, plus numerous other Christian virtues that are practiced by the church. These all witness to the presence of a loving God willing to give abundant life and bring freedom from the lies and oppression of the enemy. Satanic power always corrupts, though, and those who seek it will ultimately be destroyed because that is the enemy's real purpose behind his so-called gifts.

RESPONDING TO AN INFECTION

But what should you do if your church becomes infected with spiritual poison, or even defects to the other side, as the above patterns indicate?

My advice to Christian leaders is: Do not allow any spiritual battle to rob you of God's joy and peace and your sleep. When you do, the enemy is winning the battle. Instead, use prayer, a mighty weapon, and the encouragement of dialogue with other leaders who can offer good counsel and a godly response. Remember, a godly response means correction of error, but done with gentleness and in love.

Dwight, the senior pastor of a conservative charismatic church, used that strategy after a group of men from his church returned from some special downtown meetings with renewed enthusiasm, but also false doctrines. They began to teach that there was only one manifestation of the Godhead—the person of Jesus Christ. Sometimes He might take the form of the Father or the form of the Spirit, they said, but there is only Jesus Christ. They argued that the Trinity was an evil doctrine.

Their teaching touched a significant number of people in his church, and Dwight knew he was on the verge of a firestorm. He finally brought the other leaders of the church together, and they began to hold prayer meetings three times a week, crying out to God to change the hearts of those who had strayed from truth. In the sovereignty of God, the lies were exposed and all but three members of the group were brought back to an orthodox position about the Trinity. God also exposed the extreme excesses of the original group and showed that His power would never be demonstrated in people who were not correct in their doctrine. By gentleness and love, what could have been a fierce, divisive controversy simply resulted in the loss of three members.

That was fortunate, although, sad to say, it rarely happens that way. Satan always wants to scare a pastor and make the church leaders shudder at what's happening in their church body in a way that makes them fearful of taking action. But when you cling to the Lord and cry out to God, God often gives victory in ways no one could anticipate.

USING TOUGH LOVE

What if you are a new member (or even an older member or teacher) and learn that your church has those who do not accept the fundamentals of the faith? Then those infiltrators with a false message gain a strong position and threaten to take over?

Tough love is paramount. Be firm but never unkind. Go slowly. You may be able to minister to the infiltrators. Keep in mind that some infiltrators are well-intentioned but misled. Some may even be longtime churchgoers but not Christians. They may be fragile people; if you bend them too fast they will break. Therefore, do not pound down their throats the Bible, the gospel, or yourself. Remember the words of Paul and show compassion, "kindness, humility, meekness, longsuffering" (Colossians 3:12). Longsuffering, or patience, requires time; be committed to the process, not to a quick fix. In these situations, quick fixes usually lead to delusions.

Church divisions and potential splits can occur, but often, by following the above procedures, they can be avoided. We need to examine our own hearts. Are we trying to work in cooperation whenever possible? I think of Bernard and Shelly in this regard. They had been involved in two church splits. Moving to a different state, they joined a fairly large church. It wasn't long until they became critical of Richard, their pastor, who was teaching basic biblical truth. Bernard and Shelly began reacting to this truth because their hearts weren't right. When problems began, Pastor Richard received reports that Bernard and Shelly were spreading dissension among the people of the church. So he went to Bernard and said he would like to begin to meet with him on a weekly basis. Bernard seemed open to that strategy.

Before long, Richard's wife was meeting with Shelly on a weekly basis. Shelly revealed that Bernard had older brothers who continually put him down and told him he was worthless. His father yelled at him severely. Through much of his life he struggled with deep feelings of inferiority. It became apparent that the reason Bernard opposed church leadership was because people from his past had so wounded him.

Pastor Richard's wife received permission to tell her husband about Bernard's painful past. Later Pastor Richard decided and Bernard agreed to draw some boundaries for Bernard, and the pastor warned him gently not to cross those boundaries. This helped Bernard see clearly what was right and wrong in his critical attitude, and he responded positively. Meanwhile, the pastor affirmed Bernard with love and discipleship by telling him of that love and of his commitment to seeing Bernard grow.

A transformation occurred. The critical spirit gradually disappeared and in its place Bernard grew in his Christian life and thrived, like one of those olive trees in the Old Testament planted by a stream of water. For the last fifteen years Bernard and Shelly have faithfully served God in that local assembly.

People are not always on the side of evil. More frequently, deceived by the lies of the enemy. Whether you are a pastor or a member of a congregation, recognize your opportunity to help those who create divisions. When godly men and women come alongside and win an opponent's trust by showing love and care, divisive people can often be turned around for good. Never write someone off simply because they're not acting the way you believe a Christian should. Sometimes they're acting that way because they simply do not know the truth.

WHEN TO LEAVE A CHURCH

Still, some may ask when it's wise to stay in the battle and when it's God's will to leave. Leaving a church is not always wrong and frequently healthy. Some churches can never be redeemed because of the level of infiltration. Here are three legitimate reasons to consider leaving a church. Notice, though, there are also cautions before making the choice to break the tie with a local church.

First, doctrinal heresy is a reason to leave. We have already looked at the dangers of doctrinal heresy. Keep in mind, sometimes error can be corrected, as in the case of Pastor Dwight's church. Also, some doctrinal issues are not fundamental to your faith and can be overlooked. For example, some doctrines, such as baptism, forms of church government, the nature of the Tribulation, and the Millennium are debatable. They should not be reasons to leave a church, even though you may personally have strong opinions on these issues.

Some doctrines, though, cannot be compromised, at least in church leaders. What doctrines then must we hold to and consider serious heresies when rejected and preached by our leaders? I'd list the following:

- The virgin birth and deity of our Lord Jesus Christ.
- The blood atonement: Jesus' sacrificial death on the cross for the sins of the world.
- Salvation by grace through faith. There is only one way to be saved and it's by faith in Christ alone. If you can't get the leadership to agree to this point, nothing can possibly be gained except to try and convert those leaders to genuine faith.
- The inspiration and absolute authority of the Scriptures. Biblical infallibilty is central to evangelical belief. Only through infallable Scriptures can we know that other doctrines are true.
- The bodily resurrection of Christ. Without the resurrection, Christianity is literally a "dead" religion.
- The one-day physical return of the Lord. That Jesus is coming again should not be compromised into saying something less, i.e., "His coming is not bodily, but a spiritual coming into the hearts of His people," or some nonsense like that.
- The triunity of the Godhead. This means that Father, Son, and Spirit are all equally divine, but also distinct persons.

To deny any doctrines in the above list is to deny the cardinal teachings of orthodox Christianity.

Second, church leaders or members engaged in public sin is a reason to leave. When church leadership or pastors refuse to deal with open sin, especially among its coleaders, you've got a problem. An example might be ongoing immorality within the ranks of leadership or being tolerated in the local body of believers. Other issues could be various addictions like alcoholism, pornography, drugs, and so on. When leaders clearly sin and do not repent, or even when they allow sin to grow and flourish in their midst, it's time to consider whether this is God's person for you to follow.

Jasper was an excellent preacher and dynamic leader. But sometimes in his antics he would do things that were unorthodox. The theme of his preaching was grace, which is wonderful. However, the people in his church often wondered if he had gone too far. For instance, he often made statements like, "Salvation is of grace, only of grace. Repentance is a work, therefore repentance is not necessary for salvation." Jasper would often say that those who came to Christ on the basis of repentance were not true Christians.

This raised the eyebrows of those in his congregation who spent time in the Word. What kept people in that church was that people flocked to it in droves. It grew fantastically. All kinds of people were being "saved." The grace message that Jasper preached with his personal interpretation became very popular. Unfortunately, it was a type of Christianity that did not impact the listener's lifestyle.

One day, the news broke that Pastor Jasper and several of the elders of the church had been involved in immorality with women both in the congregation and outside of the congregation. Even more shocking was the revelation from Jasper that though this might not be in the perfect will of God, this was permissible under grace.

A group of people under wise counsel left that body and formed a new church that is flourishing today. Jasper's old church, though, has all but died.

Christians cannot tolerate overt sin in the church leadership. If the leaders refuse to admit guilt and repent, it's time to leave that church.

Third, if God has called you elsewhere, you should leave the church. Sometimes the Lord truly calls Christians to serve in another place. This may be a new job or a life transition, or for Christian leaders, including pastors, a new vocational ministry. At such a time the ideal would be to have the church you are leaving release or send you to the new body.

Be careful, though, when you take such a direction that it is not your pride or a lust for personal glory driving you. But if in your heart of hearts you perceive God wants you in another church plant or situation, by all means heed that prompting.

When I was a student in Bible college and assisting as a youth pastor in a rapidly growing church in a city in the Midwest, the senior pastor and I would pray together every Saturday afternoon. Often we prayed about all kinds of places and situations and, to my amazement, as we would pray about other countries, tears would drip down his face, especially when we prayed for Spain. As we were praying, I often felt rather unspiritual because I did not have a burden for Spain at all.

After several months of this, I began to wonder what was going on in his life. I found out when one day he announced that God had called him and his wife as missionaries to Spain. He soon raised all his financial support, went to Spain, and was used of God to found a number of Bible-believing churches.

The church that I was part of at that time happily released him to go to another part of the world because they also had seen his "burden" for Spain.

I believe that just as my pastor friend was called of God to serve in another part of His world, so God calls us at times to serve Him in other places, other cities, other churches. The only caveat I'd offer is that you be sure of your call. But if God is speaking to you, like He was to my pastor, then move ahead at full speed. You have nothing to fear except stepping out of the will of God by not doing it.

WRONG REASONS TO LEAVE

Many transfers from one local body to another have nothing to do with the above reasons. People conjure up all kinds of reasons they must leave their church that are not legitimate or God-led. Here is a list of the reasons I often hear when someone leaves their church:

- "I wasn't getting fed." Proverbs says, "To a hungry soul every bitter thing is sweet" (27:7). As long as the Word of God is being preached—accurately and with insight—spiritual feeding is taking place.
- "God is telling us to leave." How can you be sure God is telling you this? Is it because of conflict you're running away from? Or problems that you could be part of fixing? God is not the "author of confusion." If God is truly telling you to leave, the message will be confirmed over time; your leaving will not be sudden or in response to anger or done in revenge.

• "The people at my church do not like, appreciate, use, understand, or care about me." This is a common complaint. Maybe you need to take steps to get involved.

The enemy loves it when the saints go church hopping. The instability and overreaction of those sheep who leave the flock at the slightest provocation have broken many pastors' hearts.

The church of Corinth remains a great example of a church with problems where the people refused to give up. Paul took sixteen chapters to rebuke the church for sixteen major problems, but the Holy Spirit never told anybody to go anywhere except the man living in immorality with his stepmother (mentioned in 1 Corinthians 5).

One should always take the matter of changing churches seriously. The Lord adds to the body as He chooses. Each local church is precious to the Lord. Beware when a bitter saint from the church down the road enters your doorway. Unless he is released by his church and led by the Lord, he may bring with him far more than you care to handle. Some who come may not even be Christians.

Remember, the local church needs you. As the apostle Paul wrote, it is "the pillar and ground of the truth." Find one you can support, where the doctrine adheres to the Word of God and leaders and pastors are above moral reproach. Serve there with gladness, and you will find spiritual strength, support, and training in the spiritual battle.

CHAPTER SIXTEEN

THE POWER
OF PRAYER,
LOVE, AND
COMPASSION

If the church is a major spiritual battleground, subject to attack by Satan and his supporters—and it is, as we've seen in the previous two chapters—God's people need to be ready for conflict. Whether the battle occurs over false doctrine, factions, immoral behavior, or some other issue, church members need to be ready.

How can you as a church member or leader repel Satan's influence? Here are three strategies for winning the spiritual battles in our churches. As we consider each, let's remember that Satan, the great deceiver, who masquerades even as an angel of light, will offer attractive situations for churches and their leaders. We must be wise to repel his efforts.

The first strategy is to pray for your church. Prayer is a powerful weapon, and the saints—all born-again believers—are urged to pray always for all things, even when fully clothed with the armor of God. (See Paul's injunctions in Ephesians 5:13, 18 and 1 Thessalonians

5:17.) When men and women of God unite within the church to pray, prayer makes a difference in their lives and in the world.

THE POWER OF PRAYER

The power of such prayer struck home to me in this rather common situation: a normal prayer meeting in a little church. One night as the pastor received prayer requests, Darlene raised her hand. "Our daughter Fay is living in immorality with a man she is not married to," she said. "She's a carnal Christian and has become bitter and rebellious and has shown this through her immorality. We are not in a position to touch her life because my husband and I cannot allow her to live in our home if she wants to live like this. We are in agreement to ask this body to pray for her, though, and I plead with you to do this." Darlene added that Fay had come to church since childhood and, in Darlene's words, "Fay knows better than how she is living."

The pastor, a godly man, responded: "In the Bible there are examples of God putting a hedge around someone. God placed a hedge around Job's children, and Gomer, Hosea's wife. Tonight let's pray and see if God may be pleased to put a hedge around this young woman named Fay."

The little congregation slipped to their knees and stepped into the throne room of God. God soon answered and put a hedge around this young woman's life. Three weeks later her father received a call. Fay said, "Dad, I don't know what is happening, but for the past three weeks it seems like there is a wall around me. I can't touch anyone. No one can reach through the wall to touch me. Dad, I want to come home. Would you let me?"

Fay made the trip, and the next Sunday she gave that testimony to the whole church. Now, several years later, Fay is married to an outstanding young man, is the mother of several young children, walks in fellowship with the Lord, and serves faithfully through her local church.

I have to ask: What if that church had not prayed? What if those at the meeting had prayed, but God had not answered because of other sin in the body?

The truth is they did pray and God heard. He answered with the kind of power it takes to stop the enemy. That's the kind of prayer I myself pray to see in our churches today.

WHY WE DON'T PRAY

The theme of prayer runs through the Bible like a silver cord. Despite that truth, saints in the church do not pray today as they ought. There are many reasons, but the main reason is the simplest: Believers are too lazy to take time to pray. It takes energy and discipline to pray; but to not pray, and not to pray regularly, runs against the command to "pray without ceasing" (1 Thessalonians 5:17).

Sometimes believers don't pray for the needs of their church because they are afraid to pray. We are to come boldly (not fearfully) to the throne of grace, according to Hebrew 4:16, but at times I find Christians who fail to pray because they're afraid God might start to work in their church and they might have to do something! Again, such fear traces back to laziness.

Then there are those believers who do not believe prayer will have an impact. "How can my prayers make any difference?" they ask. They are examples of James's statement, "You do not have because you do not ask" (James 4:2). These are in some ways the worst sort of members, as deep down they may not know God. Or they may doubt that God would be concerned about their little church—or even their big church that seems to be doing just fine with all its programs. Such church members forget that their church, like them, is not dealing with a schedule or an agenda of activities, but with a spiritual journey that Satan wants to detour.

At other times I've seen pastors who do not encourage their people to pray. Maybe they have a belief problem themselves, or they have prayed in the past and saw no change occur. They've given up. Part of equipping the flock, though, is teaching the people how to pray.

Another common reason is that some believers do not know how to pray. Even Jesus' disciples didn't, so it's nothing to invoke shame. However, people who aren't sure what they can pray about or what methods to use should just say one thing: "Please teach me!"

Then there are those whom Satan has hindered in their prayer lives. When we commit sin, or treat our family or spouse wrong, our prayers will be hindered, according to 1 Peter 3:7. To remove that barrier, clearly sins must be confessed and forsaken.

PRAYING BECAUSE WE LOVE HIM

Whatever the reasons for lack of prayer, the truth is prayerlessness is symbolic of a heart shift away from God. Our Lord Jesus Christ knows that a change of affection is really a transfer of affection from God to self or someone else. Before the resurrected Jesus reappeared to His disciples at the Sea of Galilee, Peter decided to fish there. He told six other followers of Jesus, "I am going fishing." Peter was saying, "I've got to do something; nothing else is happening. Let's go fishing! Maybe permanently!" Following his lead, the other disciples said, "We are going with you also" (John 21:3). In effect, that day Jesus lost over half of his disciples to the fishing industry!

The next morning, after breakfast with Jesus, the Master asked Peter the question that would force him to examine his heart: "Simon, son of Jonah, do you love Me more than these?" (John 21:15). What did he mean, "more than these?" Answer: More than these *fish*. One might think Jesus meant the other disciples, but from the context it was fish and fishing! Jesus was asking Peter which he preferred, Jesus or fish!

When we stay connected with Christ through prayer and His Word, it's then we become a praying church. Jesus said, "If you abide in Me, and My words abide in you, you will ask what you desire, and it shall be done for you" (John 15:7).

The greater God and His love become in our hearts, the better we will be able to gain His perspective on our situations and the problems that we face.

SPIRITUAL WARFARE OR DISCIPLINE?

A non-praying church never knows what God is doing in their midst. The Lord could be sending chastisement or judgment and the members, due to a lack of intimacy through lack of prayer, may not respond in repentance. Some churches react wrongly to circumstances, thinking the enemy is attacking, when in reality he has already sidelined the church's ministry through the people's lack of prayer. A common error is to label as "spiritual warfare" everything bad that happens to a church. Spiritual warfare does occur in many cases, but so does God's discipline. If we mistake discipline for Satan's attack, God will not be able to get our attention and call us to repent.

In this context, I think of Pastor Marshall. He went the normal college and seminary route. He came to his first church with a master of divinity degree in his pocket but little experience. He could not easily recognize the church's spiritual condition. He soon learned that this one-time large church had shrunk to a small one; that though live (barely), it needed a resurrection if it wanted to accomplish anything in the name of Jesus Christ.

Pastor Marshall learned the greatest problem was the community's opinion of the church. It was bad, and no one was about to become a part of it. He also realized a tremendous amount of discouragement had infected the body itself.

Seeking God and reading the Scriptures for answers, Pastor Marshall came to an understanding of James's text, "You do not have because you do not ask." He also discovered God had something in store for this church if its members would pray.

He and his wife were convinced God wanted them there, so they both began to pray, crying out to God. Pastor Marshall poured out the needs of the people before the throne of grace. As time went on, members began to notice something different about him and to catch the vision for prayer. They began opening the doors of the church at 5:30 in the morning for prayer. And the members came! Five mornings a week people came to the altar throughout the morning to pray. Through prayer, they recognized their cold hearts and God's readiness to embrace those who returned to Him.

Another discovery followed: The members found if they prayed for an hour before a church business meeting the meeting would last five or ten minutes! Now that's the kind of answer I can relish!

At the same time, prayer grew in their worship on Sunday mornings. Visitors sensed a unique spirit of God in that place. The church began to grow and the prayers continued. The church bounded from a mere fifty people to two hundred in the first year. Now, ten years later, the church averages more than sixteen hundred simply through God's leadership in prayer.

When I asked for the meaning he saw behind it, Pastor Marshall told me, "Prayer is the lubricant that lubricates the machinery of the church. Not praying is like not breathing. Christians die! But when God builds into the hearts of our people a passion for prayer, we live."

I can't emphasize it enough. If you have problems or your church has problems, pray. God will answer, and you will live again—joyously and fully!

THE POWER OF LOVING THE LORD JESUS

Beyond prayer is another strategy crucial to a church's success in battling the enemy: love for Christ. "I have this against you," Jesus told the Ephesians church, "that you have left your first love" (Revelation 2:4).

Many believers wear their faith like a second layer of skin covering a rebellious or apathetic heart. They excuse their apathy in the name of the Spirit of God, saying, "Look what the Spirit's doing! How can we be anything but in the center of God's will?" Others excuse themselves by saying they present the Scriptures to others, so how can they be out of the will of God?

Certainly committed believers who love the Lord Jesus reside in both groups. But we must examine our own hearts and make sure the Lord Jesus remains our first love. The church of Ephesus had forsaken her first love. God called her to "remember" and "repent" or the results could be fatal. Churches disband every week, many dying out because they left their first love; they forgot to love Jesus.

RESTORING A LOVE FOR JESUS

When such a love is lacking, church leaders, especially pastors, can be used by God to restore this "first love." Reed Thompson (not his real name) was enthusiastic when a church that he was very fond of— one he had attended as a youth—issued him a call to come as senior pastor after he had completed seminary. Saved at a young age and having grown up in an evangelist's home, Reed had a zeal for preaching God's good news. He graduated from the seminary and could not wait to get there.

Things went well until he began to sense a severe coldness in that church. It was a deadness toward the Lord and spiritual things. The attendance had not shrunk notably, but the spiritual life of the church had declined sharply. It had been quite a few years since he had been there as a younger man, and he was shocked by this change.

He began reading up on what had taken place in the church since he had attended. He learned that the church's two previous pastors had been dismissed by the congregation. As he looked at the allegations, he could not find any substance to the charges.

Calling the two former pastors, Reed talked with them and found that they had been hurt severely by the church. Slowly and carefully he brought this to the attention of several elders, saying perhaps these men had been unjustly dismissed. The board decided to call a full meeting of the elders. Significantly, the church leaders agreed and admitted their error: They had dismissed these two men without cause.

After a time of prayer, Pastor Thompson and the congregation asked each of the former pastors to come back for an important visit. The pastors were asked to preach in the Sunday service. After the service, before the whole church, the chairman of the elders asked both former pastors' forgiveness for the unjust dismissals and then they gave each one a year's salary. That act showed their love of Christ for the two Christian brothers, and it caused Christ's love to come afresh upon the church.

Pastor Thompson told me, "Ken, you would not believe what has happened in our church. The blessing of God has come upon our people. The bitterness and the spiritual coldness that was once in their hearts is gone. We have a people who are in love with Jesus Christ. It's like the church at Ephesus in the book of Revelation that needed to repent of leaving its first love. We did that, and we as a people are different. It has only been by the grace of God. I am thrilled to be the shepherd of this, God's flock."

There are many reasons one can fall out of love with their "first love." This is only one: failing to honor a church's leader or reacting unfairly, without love or mercy. But it's a serious one. Sometimes whole churches need to repent of past mistakes and make restitution in order to show their real love for Jesus.

I remember Pastor Garth, who after reading several books and spending some time with me in my office, recognized that his own church and family were confronting spiritual warfare issues. He decided he would take a stand against the real enemy. He began taking warfare seriously and dealing with problems in his church from that perspective.

Sometime later, he told me, "Since that time with you I have not had a week go by that someone has not come to freedom in Jesus Christ. The vast difference it has made is the quality of the love people have for Jesus Christ. Where there were resentments and grudges, there is now repentance and love. It is worth the price to stand with Jesus Christ against the enemy in truth."

To that I can only say a very hearty "Amen."

THE POWER OF COMPASSION

In all churches, the people and the pastor not only need ministering to in order to prepare them for spiritual battle, but a church also must minister to broken people. This is the strategy of compassion, and it too repels Satan's influence.

Sadly, many of our clients report to us, "Our local church doesn't care about us. The pews of our church are filled with hurting people and the leadership doesn't care about their healing." They will go on to explain that in their church, numbers is the name of the game. The wounded learn quickly that if they don't fit into the flow of church life, they can go elsewhere to worship. This is a tactic of Satan, I believe, to destroy the real ministry of the church.

When a church takes warfare seriously and works to meet real needs, spiritual healing results.

Ultimately, the question for all of us in the church is: Are we allowing the world in any way to compete with our love for Christ? This is precisely what the enemy wants to accomplish: get us in the church to put our eyes on the things of the world rather than the things of Christ. When he accomplishes that, a church is dead; it is through with ministry. Only by raising up a contingent of spiritual warriors is there ever any hope of turning back the power of the enemy. But when God does that, His victory is assured.

I know a Baptist church in Minnesota that stood. It stood against evil in the community. It stood against the vile acts of men—the homosexual community. But this church stood with compassion and love—and prayer. Such responses made the surrounding community take note.

The pastor had spoken publicly against a "gay rights ordinance," which was actually a special rights measure appearing on the city ballot. The church took as its mandate the Scripture "And have no fellowship with the unfruitful works of darkness, but rather expose them. For it is shameful even to speak of these things which are done by them in secret" (Ephesians 5:11–12). When the community voted down the ordinance, the persecution began. The church was pelted with stones, the windows were broken, the church was vandalized and twice set on fire.

Then the attacks became personal. Hate mail was sent to the church. The pastor's car was destroyed by people beating it with chains. People broke into the pastor's house, killed his dog, cut it to pieces, put parts of the dog upon the children's beds, and left notes that vowed that this would happen to the children if the pastor did not change his stand against evil in the community. Someone shot at the pastor's wife a "high-powered pistol," according to police who later recovered spent bullets.

Meanwhile, church attenders returned to the church parking lot to find their tires had been slashed during services.

Throughout this time, the pastor and his family always responded in love. No one could spot bitterness in anyone in the family. At the same time, the large church, with almost two thousand members, actively reached out to the homosexual community with the love of Christ.

How could the pastor, his family, and church members show such love? Being human, they did feel fear and anxiety, the pastor later acknowledged. It would have been easier to quit. But they stood because of the power of God. The church leaders and pastor determined to pray more. They especially prayed for those who would "revile and persecute [them], and say all kinds of evil against [them] falsely for

[Christ's] sake" (Matthew 5:11). At times they would have all-night prayer meetings with believers coming to pray for an hour or several hours. Some prayed all night. (Ironically, the greatest pain came not from the homosexual community, but from evangelicals who condemned the church as being unloving. Those critical Christians forgot that exposing sin in the power of the Holy Spirit is actually an act of love.)

Watching the church's loving response, some of those caught in the homosexual lifestyle were being set free; they found Christ as their Savior. Today that church continues to grow. Homosexuals are still repenting and becoming believers in Christ. Many have seen the power of God and want to experience it themselves. Several of the former homosexuals who received the Lord testified that what brought them to Christ was the loving responses by those in the church. They went on to say they were never publicly disdained or called names, but rather treated as people who in spite of their sin are precious to the Lord.[1]

I believe our world is looking for Christians who will stand strongly for Him—but always with love and compassion, modeling the same love Jesus has demonstrated for them. That is how we repel Satan's influence and attract others to the kingdom.

BEYOND THE DECEPTIONS

PART FIVE

1. What part of the whole armor of God does the local church represent?

2. What place does the local church have in your life? Do you have a local assembly you call home?

PART SIX

WE HAVE
CHRIST'S
HEALING

THE GREAT DECEPTION...
AND THE TRUTH

SATAN'S LIE: "You're a victim; there is no hope."
(See Ecclesiastes 2:22–23.)

GOD'S TRUTH: *"He has anointed Me to preach the gospel to the poor, . . . to set at liberty those who are oppressed"* (Luke 4:18).

CHAPTER SEVENTEEN

THE WOUNDS
OF ABUSE

Child abuse has been found to be a more common occurrence than once thought. And it takes place in more forms than once thought. Beyond physical and sexual abuse, we now know verbal abuse can be just as damaging. Daryl suffered from verbal and physical abuse more than fifty years ago, and the effects remind us of the long-term consequences. His eventual triumph over those consequences also reminds us of the spiritual victory that can result.

When Daryl's older brother was sent to school, Daryl's mother sent him along, thinking he was smart and could carry on with the others in the first-grade class, even though he was only four. Anna Smithfield (not her real name) was just out of high school when she became Daryl's teacher. A two-month summer teaching course was all the formal teacher's training she had. In addition, the new teacher brought with her a childhood in an abusive home. Of course, more than fifty years ago abusive experiences or tendencies were never mentioned or even considered in the hiring and employing of teachers or anyone else.

Daryl at age four was not mentally or emotionally ready for the demands of school, even though he was exuberant and bright. It was soon obvious he could not perform as well as other first graders, but Miss Smithfield was determined to make a special case out of him. Instead of asking his parents to wait until he was older before they put him in school, she had him stay in class, determined to teach him if it was "the last thing I ever do."

The challenge of teaching a four-year-old in the first grade would be tough enough for any seasoned teacher. But in Miss Smithfield's case, with abuse as her only disciplinary tool to compel children to obey, she began levying terrible consequences on Daryl when he failed to give the answers she wanted. Those consequences included lots of verbal abuse. She frequently put a dunce cap on his head and mocked him by parading him in front of the other students and calling him "stupid," "idiot," and other things. When even this didn't bring him into line, harsh spankings and other physical consequences followed.

This went on for the first six years of Daryl's education in the one-room school of olden days. How did Daryl respond to this treatment? Like most children in such a situation, he did not turn his anger toward his teacher. Instead, he turned it toward himself, believing he was born stupid, would never amount to anything, and was the "worst case ever" of "intellectual inability."

ABUSE THAT LED TO ANGER

Fortunately, Daryl escaped that teacher a few years later when she left teaching to get married. He excelled in school from that point on, earning several degrees, including a Ph.D. To his amazement, he possessed an acute business sense that made him very successful financially. He married a wonderful woman and raised happy, disciplined children who also grew into achieving adults. But successful as he was, Daryl fought an internal battle with anger that often threatened to rise to the surface in violent, curse-spewing outbursts. Purely out of self-discipline and raw determination, he never let the internal battle show outwardly except in private moments when no one was watching. Even then, his anger remained subdued and controlled, though he seethed with rage inside.

This anger, though, manifested itself in another way: He developed a deeply critical spirit toward people in positions of authority. The government, teachers, policemen, and others became the objects of well-shot barbs of hatred and revulsion. Daryl had nothing good to say about anyone who held such a position.

As we worked through this history in my office and then prayed together, the Lord spoke to Daryl's heart in a way I've often seen but which always stuns me at the speed with which it can happen. God revealed to Daryl that he had walled off this tremendous anger toward his grade-school teacher, pretending that feeling never really developed, but manifesting the feeling in this solidly critical spirit. Through the years, the enemy told him, "You are angry at yourself (which he was) and at God who created you stupid, but not at your teacher." Daryl remembered Miss Smithfield, herself quite deceptive and elusive, had a pet phrase she used before she physically or mentally abused Daryl. She'd gravely say, "Daryl, this is for your own good. I am only doing this for you because I care about you. I really believe this will help you do better."

This, in some ways, made her a saint in Daryl's mind. He believed that teacher so completely that the idea he was stupid, worthless, and useless stayed with him long into a successful adulthood.

During our session, the Lord suddenly revealed the true source and effect of his anger. Sitting there, Daryl said, "You mean I'm not stupid? My teacher was wrong?"

It was so obvious to me and everyone else that it was almost funny to see this successful, disciplined, and intelligent man saying such a thing. But that is the power of Satan's lies. They imbed themselves in our mental machinery against all evidence to the contrary.

I told Daryl that this belief resulted from his teacher's abuse, not because it was real or true. Satan had used the teacher to convince Daryl he was stupid; Satan had convinced Daryl that God had created him that way.

For several minutes he sat there confused and amazed as he mulled over this monumental fact. In the end, though, he saw it was true. "I am not stupid. God has given me abilities." Instantly, the confusion disappeared. All the anguish and bitterness were released in a quiet prayer of confession as he sought God and thanked Him for opening his eyes to the truth.

After this confession, he immediately asked the Lord to forgive him for all the criticism he'd levied against others and for his bitterness. At that point, it was as if a dam broke in his soul. The simple prayer resulted in peace and joy flooding his heart, so that a new tenderness toward others gripped him. In only weeks, everyone in his family wondered what had happened. Gentle, kind words fell from his lips and the critical spirit disappeared.

What had happened? The lie—formed in the verbal and physical punishment by a teacher—was exposed and he was free. He felt release from fifty years of bondage, not because of me as his counselor, but because God had brought light and life to him in a way he'd never experienced before. Daryl often used the word "healed" in explaining to others what had happened to him: "I've been healed."

Today Daryl enjoys a deeper walk with the Lord and has a more effective ministry to the body of Christ than ever before.

THE SOURCE OF HEALING

Real healing came into Daryl's life as the Lord revealed what was hidden; namely, a deep-rooted hostility and anger toward a teacher who abused him almost daily. Rarely does a small child ask, "What is wrong with the person in charge?" Instead, the child asks, "What is wrong with me?"

Such abuse is all too common in our lie-bombarded world. A huge part of spiritual warfare is not knocking back the bastions of Satan, but helping his victims see the deceptions of the Evil One and directing them to true healing and hope in Christ.

Healing is the best word for describing what happens to patients who have been lied to by the enemy. They were "sick" in the sense that they believed the lies that let them color everything they did and believed. Their conduct and behavior were "tainted" by the disease that the lies spread in their lives. For many of us, healing is the answer.

What happens when you're healed from a sickness? When germs invade your body, they weaken it and then take over. If they're given freedom to proliferate, they can render a patient bedridden and eventually destroy his very life. Similarly, when lies attack our minds and we accept them, we can become dysfunctional and sinful, and eventually those lies can destroy relationships at home and work. Healing happens when an antibiotic or drug—in this case, truth—is put into the body (mind and heart), kills the germs (lies), and allows the body to heal (grow spiritually and emotionally).

That's the essence of spiritual warfare. Germs have invaded our bodies, bent on killing us. But God gives us His powerful antibiotic —truth—and the lies are destroyed.

In this chapter, we'll explore the power we have in our Lord to find healing, hope, and refreshment, even in the midst of circumstances so terrible one might be tempted to think the only answer was suicide.

THE IMPORTANCE OF INNER HEALING

In my counseling ministry I seek to help clients enter into the healing process and to give the Holy Spirit room to work in lives that have been badly battered. Emotional, mental, and spiritual healings are in many ways far more significant than physical healing. Most people, when taken ill even with a terminal disease, can work through it with joy in their hearts and an expectation of seeing Jesus. But depressed, broken, beaten, and battered souls have no peace, hope, joy, or even love. They are the walking dead. Through the Spirit it is my task to try to illuminate the path to healing through Christ.

Marla walked that path after her pastor sent her to me because of clinical-level depression.

"I have been depressed for forty years," she told me up front. She had come because she was told to. Early on in our counseling, she said, "I don't want to be here. I wouldn't be here if my pastor did not demand I come and see you."

As we began to visit, I learned that she grew up in an abusive home where she was neglected, and she had never bonded with her father or mother. She was the child they called "the mistake."

After the first three-hour session in which I laid out for her the reality of spiritual warfare, though, she jarred me when she said, "I think you are quite stupid. As a matter of fact, the idea that the enemy can oppress someone who is a Christian is ridiculous. When God saved me, He put a shield around me that is impenetrable to anyone except the Holy Spirit. My depression is simply biochemical; there is no spiritual element involved here. So when you tell me I need to look at my life and my attitude, I honestly think it's ridiculous. You are one of the most stupid people I have ever met."

As she left, I asked the Lord for unique grace to make it through the next two days; Marla had come to our offices from out of town for three daily sessions, each three hours in duration. "Lord," I prayed, "if it would please You, would You please cause the enemy to overstep his boundaries in Marla's life in a nonharmful way." (Sometimes even we "compassionate" counselors pray prayers like that!)

That evening she walked into her hotel room, and after she had settled down for the evening she heard a voice say, "You are right; Ken Copley is truly a charlatan. He is one of the most stupid people I have ever met, to say nothing of you. So you see, Marla, there is no hope for you; you might as well take your life."

She had never heard a voice before, and now she remembered my words that her battle was merely spiritual. *I think this might be the enemy Ken Copley is talking about,* she told herself.

The next day she came back with a whole new attitude. For the first time she was willing to pray, cry out to God, and ask the Spirit to show her areas in her life where she was believing lies. The Spirit of God dealt first with the issue of whether she was a mistake on the part of her parents in conceiving her. I showed her she was fearfully and wonderfully made; she was not the child of the worthless, but a child of the living God. The Holy Spirit and the Scriptures began to assure her heart that God had a plan for her. She confessed sins that dealt with her attitude, her rebellion, and her critical spirit. Truly repentant, she asked God to take back ground she had given to Satan concerning all these things.

Wonderfully, her depression lifted. She decided I wasn't so stupid after all, and three years later she wrote me: "I have never again entered that deep black hole of depression. I know God loves me, I know

He is with me, I know He has ordered the events of my life and is sovereignly in control. I trust implicitly in Him."

Today Marla is actively serving the Lord. But it came at a price; she had to humble herself, cry out to Him, and receive God's deliverance.

OF WHAT THEN DO PEOPLE NEED TO BE HEALED?

There are many afflictions, but the primary ones are from the inner brokenness, wounds, and crushed spirit that have been inflicted on many in our world. Wounds may come from childhood abuse. They often result from our own sinful acts. Wounds may also be caused by authorities overstepping boundaries, as in Daryl's case. Often they are the result of us believing lies that have been placed in our hearts by the world, the flesh, or the devil.

Many of my clients become upset when they realize that the enemy has attacked them. But the thing we need to remember is that the devil never kicks a dead horse. If you're feeling the kicks, you're still alive, and you can still experience healing and hope in Christ. That is the promise I always make to my clients. "If you honestly seek Christ in the midst of your terrible situation, you will be surprised at the amazing things He will do to help!"

HEARING GOD SPEAK— THROUGH SCRIPTURES AND THE HOLY SPIRIT

How exactly does Jesus help us and move us toward genuine healing?

I believe genuine healing comes largely through Jesus communicating with us personally to reveal the truth in our hearts and expose the lies we've let control our lives. In the book *Experiencing God,* Henry Blackaby wrote, "If I do not know when God is speaking, I am in trouble at the heart of my Christian life."

Being able to "hear God" is the primary point at which Satan attacks. He wants to dull our "faith sense" that enables us to hear God's voice and learn the truth we need to apply in any given situation. Blackaby goes on to say, "God never will lead you in opposition to His written Word."[1]

Occasionally, people come to me who believe God wants them to do things contrary to Scripture. They are supposed to unload their anger on their family as a means of "venting." Or they believe they should hurt someone physically who has hurt them. But my counsel is always "What does God's Word say?" If something we "hear" in our hearts is contrary to that, then we can be sure that is not the voice of God. As Blackaby noted, "When God speaks to me, revealing what He is about to do, that revelation is my invitation to adjust my life to God. Adjustments prepare me for obedience. I cannot stay where I am and go with God. God's greatest single task is to get His people adjusted to Himself." At that point, he made an insightful warfare statement: "The only way Satan can affect God's work through me is when I believe Satan and disbelieve God."[2]

I believe the Lord Jesus Christ speaks by the Holy Spirit using the Word, and that by the prompting of the Spirit He gives mental pictures both through the Word and by His "still small voice" that every child of God can hear within his heart if he chooses. In all such communication, God never adds to His Word, nor does He ever contradict it.

This is the means by which He heals and opens a heart to the truth. Who then does Jesus heal? We will answer that question in the next chapter.

CHAPTER EIGHTEEN

HELP AND HEALING FROM THE GREAT PHYSICIAN

Healing from abuse requires forgiveness. Granting forgiveness is often not easy to do; it seems doubly difficult in the case of abuse. There has been an injustice; the perpetrator has inflicted hurt, even pain; and the consequences typically are long lasting. How can someone forgive?

The answer: only by the supernatural grace of God. Indeed, He forgave so that we might be able to forgive as well (Ephesians 4:32).

In the previous chapter, recall that Daryl suffered abuse at the hands of his teacher, Miss Smithfield. Remember that this teacher had been poorly trained and was abused herself. While that doesn't excuse Miss Smithfield's conduct, it gave some of the understanding necessary for Daryl to honestly forgive her. Like Jesus said, "Father, forgive them for they know not what they do."

Jesus understood that the very people who crucified Him were not understanding criminals, but ignorant savages. Had they really understood whom they were nailing to the cross and seen the true motives of the leaders of the Jews, their guilt would have multiplied. But their ignorance and their own victimization at the hands of others makes their actions less malevolent.

Daryl recognized this about the woman who abused him, and he could forgive her a bit more easily than if she had been a raging serial abuser who knew exactly what she was doing. He could honestly say, "Lord, forgive her, for she knows not what she did."

JESUS HEALS HURTS
FROM ABUSE BY AUTHORITIES

Some might say, "That's a cop-out. She's responsible for what she did!" Yes, and those in authority must be especially careful not to misuse their authority, whether they are teachers, law officers, or parents. But in this case, her guilt was out of ignorance, not intent. Scripture itself supports the idea that when we sin in ignorance, our punishment before God will be less severe (see Luke 12:47–48).

On the other hand, no abuse is easy to forgive. For Daryl, simply speaking the words were difficult. When I spoke to him of forgiveness, he deliberated. I prayed that God would speak to his heart, and that was ultimately what happened. I find that it always takes Christ's intervention, through counsel, insight, and great compassion, to enable any Christian to take the steps of forgiveness that Daryl did. But the fact is that he did, and it set him free.

HEALING AFTER ABUSE: KNOWING THE TRUTH

We will not always understand the reason for abuse. At times, the person's actions may have been selfish, an overuse of power at one's disposal. At other times, there may have been mitigating factors, but we must still love. And there are times when the specific reason will never be known, or the abuser was confused as to why he or she acted so wrongly. It matters little; one does not need to know the perpetrator's motive in order to forgive. Through His grace and forgiveness the Lord enables us to forgive, even as He commands us (Ephesians 4:32).

When authorities—those who are in charge and whom we often

respect—abuse us as children, that abuse can make us think strange things. We may think we indirectly caused the abuse—our stupidity, our disobedience, our failure made the person attack us. Satan lies to abuse victims; he tells them those very things that keep them mired in confusion and fear. It is up to counselors and those in the church to reveal the truth. As always, truth and love together can bring healing.

I saw this in Harley when he visited my office. It was difficult for him to speak because he kept sobbing almost out of control. He unfolded his story one layer at a time as he told about growing up in an abusive home. It was a familiar scene: His father was an alcoholic —an abuse victim himself. Usually he would spank Harley, but at other times he would get in his face and scream. Typically he would yell cruel, cutting things: "You are a piece of garbage; you are utterly stupid."

Harley said, "It was not the spankings that wounded me. It was the screaming that wounded my soul. The yelling and what he yelled were what lodged so deeply in my being."

As we prayed, the Holy Spirit brought the lies to the surface, which we were able to dispel with God's truth. Step by step, Harley came to the freedom that is only found in Jesus Christ. The beautiful thing in it all was that God took Harley and put him into a loving local assembly of men who were willing to listen to him, encourage him, and help him mature in Christ. As God brought the truth about being made in God's image and being a child of God into Harley's life, he found true healing. Harley says, "I am not the same person I was a year ago. I know who I am in Jesus Christ. I am very glad to be alive and to know I have a place assigned by God in His kingdom."

I have never in all my counseling years encountered a man or woman who was bitter and wounded because of biblical discipline, which includes spanking. However, I have come across many who have been wounded deeply because they were yelled at and called names; that is not discipline at all. It is verbal abuse that attacks the child's very identity. As parents we have a responsibility to treat children as they were created, "fearfully [that is respectfully] and wonderfully made" by the Creator.

JESUS HEALS WOUNDS FROM SEXUAL ABUSE

Sexual abuse will create another deep wound that will require healing. As a child, Janet had been sexually molested. She spent much time as a child with her unmarried uncle who treated her "special," which was his euphemism for abuse. The painful memories of that molestation were burned into her heart. Now married for more than a dozen years, Janet found it difficult to have sexual intimacy with her husband. When she would attempt to have a physical relationship with Bob, the memories would surface and she would react. Bob interpreted those reactions as rejection. This set the stage for much pain and frustration in their marriage. Recently Bob confessed to having an affair, and Janet went into a deep depression.

Bob sought counseling first, and he took responsibility for his adultery. He knew he had created Janet's depression, and he sought to win his wife's trust and rebuild a loving relationship with his children. During our counseling session, Bob broke and wept over the awfulness of his sin against God and Janet. Satan filled him with fears that she'd never forgive him, that he'd never find "true satisfaction sexually" from his wife, and that he would face even deeper emptiness for the rest of his life because God was against him.

Bob, though, confessed these lies and as he faced them, he realized they were deceptions designed to keep him from real healing. In a sudden turnaround, he shook his head and asked his wife to forgive him. He asked God to do radical amputation and cut the idols out of his heart. He prayed, "Father, I repent of the sin of adultery with (he named the woman). Please separate my body, soul, and spirit from the body, soul, and spirit of [he named the woman]."

Later, as I talked with Janet, she realized that she had to forgive her uncle and release him to the Lord. His actions had made her feel dirty, trapped, and helpless; those actions also had made her uncomfortable about having sexual relations with her husband. Bob's confession and repentance had helped, but now Janet needed to forgive her uncle and purge those lies. Eventually she prayed, forgiving her uncle. Then the Lord spoke to her heart and erased the lies that had been planted there many years before. Gone were the feelings and beliefs of being dirty, guilty, worthless, and undesirable. As she submitted to God, love, joy, and peace took the place of those former feelings and beliefs. Now Janet was able to also forgive Bob from her heart for his adultery and release him to the Lord. I watched with joy as the Lord tore down the walls of bitterness that stood between them. Their hearts connected for the first time in their married lives. Bob reports today that their intimate physical relationship reflects what God intended all along and that they are learning that they can "trust in the Lord, and do good.... Delight yourself also in the Lord, and He shall give you the desires of your heart" (Psalm 37:3–4).

WHY?

Almost daily in my counseling I hear the question asked, "Why did God let it happen?" Janet asked the Lord this question, and He gave her the answer that "I used it to bring you to Me." She told me, "It was during that awful time when I cried out to God that He saved me."

God doesn't always give an answer like that, but He did give us Romans 8:28–29—the promise that He works all things for good to those who love God and are called to His purpose. God the Father did not stop the crucifixion, but He gave us Easter. He is always able to bring good out of bad, if we'll only turn to Him in faith and trust Him to do it.

JESUS HEALS FROM THE OCCULT

Satan uses all kinds of abuse to render Christians ineffective. One is direct—right out of his hand: occult involvement. Daisy grew up in a family that was heavily involved in the occult. She told me, "All throughout my childhood I was deathly afraid of my mom. She was an angry, cold, distant person who constantly [physically] abused me. It was as if she took out all her rage on me. My father was the only doctor in our small town and was never home."

What was most horrifying about her case was that, as a child, at times she could actually see a demonic presence. "As a toddler I distinctly remember evil beings coming through the window to harass me. These beings would hover near my crib until I lost consciousness due to fear."

Amazingly enough, God entered this arena unbidden.

"Around that same time, God, in His great love, brought a godly Christian family into our neighborhood. Through their grandmother I first heard about the Lord Jesus Christ. I was too young to understand the depth of Christ's message, but I fully understood that there was Someone who loved me unconditionally."

Daisy listened to these folks and found in them a source of comfort and hope. However, her situation at home did not change.

"The conditions of my family and childhood worsened as I grew older. I became suicidal in my adolescence, and my mother threatened to commit me to a mental hospital. I got the message loud and clear that I was crazy. Seeking help, I began attending a nearby church. However, this church did not preach the Gospel, and its social message did not soothe my conscience nor bring peace to my fearful heart.

"Finding no hope in hollow 'religion,' I turned to drinking and sex," Daisy said. She found that the only love she knew was abuse, so when she met a charming but abusive young man (named John) she thought she was in love. In 1970, the year she turned twenty-one, she accepted John's offer of marriage. But she was not happy.

"It was not long before my marriage fell apart, with my husband threatening to kill me," Daisy said. "He showed up at the hospital one day where I was being treated (for wounds he had inflicted on me) and threatened to kill my doctor. Almost immediately I filed for divorce."

The strange thing in the midst of this was the constant call of God on her heart. In the midst of her horrid situation God spoke, and she says, "I was filled with a burning desire for God. I set out on a mission to seek the Jesus Christ I had heard about when I was a young child."

After her release from the hospital and subsequent divorce, Daisy returned to wondering about what God would do with her. He answered swiftly: "A few months later my baby-sitter introduced me to a pastor's daughter who was holding Bible studies in her home. There I came to a fuller understanding of the work of Christ on the cross to free me from my sin and bondage to the evil one. There were many nights when I would stay up reading the gospel of John with my light on because of my terror of demonic spirits."

During that time, she prayed one night for Christ to come into her life, not sure He really would. Instantly, she says, "A great peace came to my heart."

Though this was a new beginning for Daisy, her journey was not at an end. She told me, "In 1986 I met a godly man in the church I was attending. After a year and four months of friendship we married. Almost immediately we had problems. We were triggering each other's woundedness. There was something that hindered our intimacy. After a very traumatic childhood and a turbulent adulthood, I had hoped that this marriage would bring the peace and joy of intimacy. However, there were things that the Lord wanted to change in me."

After her second marriage she came for counseling and there God showed her the lies of Satan that she was still believing. As these truths registered in her spirit, God gave her the power to renounce those lies and believe His truth. We continue to work together, and she recently said, "I am now finding in Christ what I was looking for in my marriage. Through the blood of Christ and the truth of Scripture I am being healed. The Lord has been faithful to keep His Word, 'You have considered my trouble; You have known my soul in adversities' [Psalm 31:7]. He is my Yeshua, the Holy One of Israel, the Lamb of God."

Daisy's case illustrates it's not a matter of drugs or human wisdom or even great compassion and love from a decent friend; no, it's the purpose and person of Christ who vanquishes the lies of the devil and takes back the ground the enemy has claimed.[1]

STEPS TO TAKE

From the counselees above and many others, I know that spiritual warfare is behind much abuse. Only by understanding it, the enemy, and the Lord can anyone truly be set free and healed.

What steps should a Christian take who has been wounded in order to find genuine healing?

1. *Recognize there is a personal God who loves you* (see John 3:16). His love can break through any darkness and help you feel not only loved but beloved, God's child and a member of His fam-

ily, wholly accepted and given all the rights of being a family member: peace, joy, hope, and the love of His people.

2. *Give your broken heart to the Lord Jesus Christ* (see Luke 4:17–21). This act of faith seals the relationship and brings you into intimate friendship with Jesus Himself.

3. *Trust Christ for promised hope and liberty* (see Luke 4:18; John 8:32, 36). Jesus will give you the hope and freedom you desire. He alone is capable.

4. *Be strengthened in the inner person by God's power* (see Ephesians 3:16–17). God alone can give us the strength to overcome.

TIME AND PATIENCE NEEDED

Healing usually happens in a context of meaningful discipleship relationships, worship, prayer support, fellowship, teaching, and growth. It's a process that often takes time and patience. We need fellowship and the friendship of loving, accepting people. Many broken people are isolated and lonely. Loneliness is to the soul what starvation is to the body.

As the testimonies in this chapter show, healing always takes place in the larger context of family, friends, and the local church. Getting involved in a God-honoring church is an essential of true healing. Don't give up on the local church. Furthermore, don't go to church to get beat up, but go to be built up. As God's truth enters the heart, the result will be spiritual wisdom that in itself will strengthen and heal that tender "inner person" that is often so vulnerable to the abuses of this world.

Louise found this out in a beautiful way. Now thirty-seven, she had been in a series of failed marriages and a number of affairs until one day she found Christ after she "decided to try Him," she said. It happened when the Lord brought a precious lady into her life at work. This Christian lady began to share Jesus with her and eventually led her to Christ.

"The problem I have now," Louise told me, "is I really don't know where I belong." She felt alone, perhaps because of her treatment as a child. Neither her father nor mother wanted her or her twin brother.

She was unwanted, and her parents had made that clear every day of her life.

I recommended a good, caring church. I even made a couple of phone calls to make the introductions for Louise. That Sunday, she later told me, it took all she had to get out of bed and actually go to church. By the grace of God, though, she made it.

As she got involved, she soon found there were a number of problems in her life that had to be resolved. For one, she had not paid income tax for several years. An attorney in the church helped her get that squared away.

The church also helped her with a mortgage on her house that was about to foreclose, and they helped her purchase a car so she could get around. She told me the greatest thing they did for her, though, was being "there . . . when I desperately needed them. If one member of the body could not meet my need they would look and find another one who could. In a matter of several months of being in the church there was a Realtor, a tax lawyer, a finance expert, a medical doctor and several sisters who came alongside to meet specific needs at that time in my life."

I believe the greatest part of her growth and healing has taken place through her local church. I urge every reader: Do not give up on the church that Jesus Christ is building. Yes, God's people still sin; yes, and they make mistakes. But if you seek out people who are truly walking with the Lord, you will inevitably find them loving, resourceful folks who will often give you the shirt off their backs to help.

THE LORD IS INVOLVED IN PHYSICAL HEALING

One might think from the above that I am only interested in emotional and spiritual healing. Let us not forget God offers physical healing as well. Though abuse typically leaves emotional and spiritual scars, sometimes abuse leaves physical scars, and sometimes the abused person forgets that Jesus is the Great Physician. In addition, sometimes we are afflicted with physical ailments and pain not related to abuse and again find ourselves asking the question of why. I believe physical healing happens—frequently—and it's something that we should honestly seek under certain conditions.

The Scriptures speak much about some diseases resulting from separation or broken relationships with God, others, and ourselves. This is one reason we need to know each other in the body of Christ in depth, not just superficially on a Sunday-to-Sunday basis.

HEALING AFTER FORSAKING SIN

I also believe some diseases are a direct result of sin. To see precisely what I mean, study the following passages: Deuteronomy 7:11–15; 28:15–22; Psalms 31:9–10; 38:3–7; Isaiah 5:13–14.

Dorothy, though, is an example of genuine physical healing. She experienced several tragic events in her life. She was bedridden for several years with chronic fatigue syndrome and fibromyalgia. She also experienced a heart attack and breast cancer before age thirty-seven. She took prescription medications for her pain, and was severely overweight. With all these conditions, she chose to become angry and bitter. She came to our clinic full of bitterness and on the verge of a breakdown.

After some time in counseling, she wrote me, "I recently repented of my bitterness and anger. The Lord set me free as I forgave those who so deeply hurt me."

She also repented of gluttony and changed her diet. Nine months after her confession of sin, she had lost eighty pounds and lowered her cholesterol by 150 points.

She told me, "With my doctor's blessing, I have stopped taking the prescription medication I had relied on for years. I now walk, run, work, and enjoy the life Christ has given me. I am no longer angry and bitter. I now have the joy of the Lord."

Such physical healing often happens as people deal with the lies and sin in their lives that Satan uses to keep them in bondage. Before her repentance, Dorothy was angry and bitter toward God, herself, and others. The effect of sustained bitterness was destroying her physically, emotionally, mentally, and spiritually. Repentance brought her God's comfort and healing.

In physical sickness as well as in anything else, we must not assign to the enemy what is not his. Many of our problems come from our willful disobedience. If a man commits adultery or visits a prostitute, he runs the risk of incurring a sexually transmitted disease. If a Christian drinks alcohol to excess or smokes cigarettes, he runs obvious physical risks. Consuming too much fat and cholesterol, or even gluttony, can result in all sorts of physical problems. In some cases, God may actually "judge" him or her by inflicting the disease because of the sin.

Likewise, psychological or spiritual sin can bring dire consequences. Uncontrolled anger can lead to a heart attack, stroke, or stomach ulcers. Bitterness and jealousy can lead to similar ailments. Worry and distrust of God in daily matters can cause one to develop heart disease or peptic ulcers.

Yet, despite the obvious problems, no matter the source, the Lord can still bring healing.

PARTIAL PHYSICAL HEALING . . . AND NO HEALING

Sometimes physical healing will be only partial; other times no healing will result. In either case, God has not been stumped. Instead He has chosen for His glory and good purposes to let the affliction remain. We need look no further than the great apostle Paul to see a godly follower of Christ continue to suffer with some unnamed "thorn in the flesh" despite "plead[ing] with the Lord three times that it might depart from me." The reason for the pain remaining? So the apostle might learn to depend on God's power in weakness, so "that the power of Christ" could be shown in him (see 2 Corinthians 12:7–9).

This was what happened with Melody. She was involved in a car wreck that changed her life. At age nineteen her car fishtailed on wet pavement, then rolled down an embankment. She was thrown from the car, and the car hit her head as it rolled down the embankment.

Her skull and the right side of her face suffered multiple fractures. The doctors told her family she would not live because of the damage to her brain. Her lungs collapsed and she was on life support. When she didn't die, the doctors said she would be in a vegetative state for the rest of her life. She remained uncommunicative and in a state of infancy for six months; then she finally began to recover. The final word from the doctors was, she would have to live in a long-term care facility. When she was ready to be released from the hospital to such a facility, her parents took Melody home against the doctor's advice.

"God gave my parents a nineteen-year-old baby," Melody later explained. "The only thing I could do was eat. My mother gave me physical therapy, taught me how to walk and talk—she even potty-trained me."

A remarkable recovery occurred during the next eighteen months. After five lengthy surgeries, Melody's face and skull were reconstructed. In the end, Melody relearned the abilities to walk, talk, sing, and work. She considers her major recovery a miracle. The only signs of her trauma are blindness in her right eye and weakness in her left side.

"The devil wanted to destroy my life," she says, "but the Lord turned this experience around in a way that gives glory to God. Because my understanding is more childlike, I am able to help more people. God has taught me to trust Him in many new ways. I'm happy to say God's glory has shown through in all my trials."

Melody believes the physical loss after the accident was helpful. "I believe God allowed me to go through this trial to teach me how to better encourage people. My trial was twofold: to bring me to a place of full surrender to the Lord, and to show forth God's glory."

Melody had heard Satan's lies shrieking in her mind, "What kind of God lets this happen to His children?" She could easily have reacted to this tragedy with bitterness and anger. Instead, she chose to walk with Christ in victory. Today, she sings in various churches as part of her family ministry team. She gives her testimony in an almost childlike voice using childlike terms. People, especially children and those who hurt, find Melody one of the most approachable people they've ever met. Everywhere she goes, she offers encouragement and the testimony that "God is with you in your pain. Look to Him and He will get you through it to victory."

Would she have learned these things apart from her accident and her agonizing medical problems? There is no answer. But the truth is that she did learn these truths through her accident and recovery and can praise God for it. That is a sign of a Christian who has done spiritual battle and found success through Christ.

Melody learned through her accident that hidden treasures often come in ugly boxes.

CALLING UPON THE GOD OF HEALING

Do you seek healing from God in some way? Has Satan buffeted you on some level like he did with the apostle Paul, placing a "thorn" in your flesh?

My word to you is that God is a God of healing. The same apostle Paul who could not fully understand his thorny affliction still accepted it, and in another letter wrote, "He who did not spare His own Son, but delivered Him up for us all, how shall He not with Him also freely give us all things?" (Romans 8:32).

God does heal the brokenhearted and the broken-bodied. I believe there is hope for anyone who will genuinely seek Christ. Perhaps your body will not achieve complete healing in this life. That doesn't matter. For you will be perfect in the next one.

And for those who have listened to Satan's lies and become entrapped and sealed in them, I say with Melody and the others in this book, you too can break out of those boxes simply by trusting Christ, learning His Word, and seeking His love at every turn of life. When that love and joy fills your heart, no tragedy can overshadow it.

BEYOND THE DECEPTIONS

PART SIX

1. If in the past you "felt" helped in dealing with an abuse but at the same time were diverted from the Cross, were you really helped?

2. Would you allow the Lord to heal you even if it meant forgiving someone, humbling yourself, forsaking a cherished sin, or genuine repentance?

PART SEVEN

WE HAVE FREEDOM!

THE GREAT DECEPTION...
AND THE TRUTH

SATAN'S LIE: "You're not free. You're a slave to sinful desires." (See Romans 7:5–6.)

GOD'S TRUTH: *"For the law of the Spirit of life in Christ Jesus has made me free from the law of sin and death"* (Romans 8:2).

CHAPTER NINETEEN

THE TRUTH
ABOUT
TRUE FREEDOM

On the 1st day of January, in the year of our Lord 1863, all per-sons held as slaves within any state or designated part of a state, the people thereof shall then be in rebellion against the United States, shall be then, thenceforward and forever [free]."

Those words are part of the great document issued by President Abraham Lincoln known as the Emancipation Proclamation. It freed all slaves in the U.S. forever, and guaranteed that slavery would nev-er again taint America's states.

In a similar way, God declared our spiritual emancipation procla-mation through the death, burial, and resurrection of our Lord Jesus Christ. The moment Jesus rose from the dead, Satan tasted utter de-feat and lost the legal right of mastery and control over the life of any believer. Satan possesses no legal, spiritual, or actual right to run our lives!

However, though the enemy has no legal right, many Christians experience his intrusion into their lives due to unresolved issues of unconfessed and unrepented sin. This is why Paul commands us to "not be entangled again with a yoke of bondage" (Galatians 5:1). Clients come to our counseling center looking for the spiritual guidance that will lead them to freedom from sin and growth in Christ. True biblical counseling seeks to equip an army for warfare against the world, the flesh, and the devil by helping them put on the spiritual armor of God (Ephesians 6:10–12).

FINDING FREEDOM WITHIN

The result of such guidance is true freedom in our inner person—a freedom to serve God and love those around us, a joy while sharing our faith, and even a smile or two. That's what Riley found out.

A pastor friend referred Riley to me, saying that Riley was hearing voices in his head. Riley had told the pastor that the voices had been speaking for the past twenty years, telling Riley he was no good, he was stupid, and he should curse God and Christ.

When Riley arrived, I had an opportunity to get acquainted with him and his wife. I asked him to explain his situation, and he said, "When I got out of the navy, I was diagnosed as being schizophrenic. I have voices that scream in my mind. With enough medication they now have them down so that it's more like a conversation in the back of my head."

It has been my experience with schizophrenics that medication sometimes takes away the voices. However, there are times when the voices are not speaking because of a biochemical problem, but rather there is an enemy behind them.

I could tell that Riley had a heart that loved God and he was sincerely seeking help, so I asked him an important question. "When did the voices start?"

"When I was in the navy," he said, "I became involved in some homosexual activity. That was the beginning of hearing voices."

I asked if he had ever asked God to forgive him for those wrongs and asked God to take back the ground he had given to Satan. To his best recollection he had not. We prayed together, I asked God to grant him repentance, and he asked the Lord to stop Satan's influence in his life. Afterward he looked at me with the most surprised look on his face and said, "This is absolutely amazing; the voices just stopped."

I praised God, and Riley asked, "What do I do now?"

I said, "Why don't you take a walk. Maybe enjoy life, enjoy the Lord. Come back in a half an hour and we will evaluate."

He took a half-hour walk and came back. When we sat down in my office again, he said, "The voices are still silent. I can't believe it."

We began to meet together on a weekly basis, and it was astonishing what would happen from week to week. After the first week he reported that his psychiatrist had said his schizophrenia had gone into total remission. He would no longer need medication. After the second week he said that for the first time in twenty years he was able to work. The third week he said for the first time in twenty years he was able to truly read the Bible, concentrating and praying on it as he went. The fourth week he shared with me that his love for his wife was growing by leaps and bounds. They now had an emotional connectedness that they had not had since the time he had met her.

It has been several years since then. Recently I received a phone call from a man who goes to Riley's church. He said, "Ken, let me give you my perspective on Riley. He works a full-time job, he is out soul winning every Thursday night, he plays on the church baseball team, and he teaches a Sunday school class. But none of that is the most amazing thing. The most amazing thing is that he grins all the time."

I could only laugh for joy at this transformation that happened as a result of a little prayer of confession and the receipt of forgiveness.

My friend said, "If I had gone through what Riley had gone through, I believe I would grin all the time, too."

Most of us will not hear voices, but many of us still need to claim our freedom in Christ. Such freedom prepares a person to go forward in truth and to stand with Jesus Christ against the world, the flesh, and the devil. Often that all begins with a single prayer of repentance.

KEYS TO SPIRITUAL FREEDOM AND GROWTH

How does anyone achieve this kind of freedom? First, one must turn his heart toward the Lord. As Solomon wrote, "Trust in the Lord with all your heart, and lean not on your own understanding; in all your ways acknowledge Him, and he shall direct your paths" (Proverbs 3:5–6). Second, he must open his heart and mind to receive the Word into every area of his life. Third, the person must be willing to obey the Lord Jesus Christ in bringing every thought and desire into conformity with Christ's truth.

I have found that the crucial point of all counseling occurs when a believer grasps his or her true identity in Jesus Christ. That happened to Stephanie, who entered my office saying she had "a screaming pain in my heart" that would not go away. I had never heard pain described like that before, so I asked her to tell me her story. She launched into it with a trembling voice that grew stronger as she talked.

She had grown up in the church and received the Lord Jesus as Savior. Her parents were not overly involved in her life. They had given her a kind of freedom she really did not need, one with no proper boundaries to protect her. As a result, she often found herself in places she really should not have been.

At age nineteen, she began to live with a young man. In due course of time she became pregnant. She asked the young man what he thought she should do. He said the decision was up to her. As a result, she went to an abortion clinic, was given some material to read over, and saw a counselor. She chose to have an abortion.

A couple of days later the truth of what she had done began to sink in. She said, "Both of us, me and my young lover, slipped into depression." A short time later, they broke up.

Some time later she shared with her father and mother that she had aborted the child and they said, "We so wish that you had told us, because we could have helped you." The great deceiver had fed her a classic lie: "Your mom and dad don't care. Don't ask for help." And the screaming in her heart became worse.

"The guilt deepened and the accusations in my heart only increased," Stephanie explained.

Immediately I turned to the issue of forgiveness from God in Christ. I knew real freedom—freedom to choose rightly and have a clear conscience—were near. I carefully walked her through the process of admission of the sin of immorality, and of taking the life of her child. She agreed and asked God to forgive her and take back the ground she had given to Satan in her soul. I listened as she prayed. Almost immediately real freedom came into her life.

We continued to talk about what God wanted for her now that she'd dealt with her heart problem. I asked the Lord to bring to her mind what lies the great deceiver had lodged in her heart. Stephanie recognized the big lie was that God would never forgive her because she had taken the life of her child. The truth was that the blood of Calvary had covered and taken away that sin.

As we talked, I sensed the Lord assuring Stephanie that her child was safe with Him and that one day in glory she would see that baby once more.

Stephanie also said that while she felt dirty and defiled, Jesus showed her she was pure and holy and righteous and clean because of His work on the Cross.

For a long time, she prayed and dedicated her life to Christ. After several counseling sessions, she told me, "I feel that God has healed me and cleansed my life of every stain of my sinful past. I really want to do His will daily and live my life for Him."

That commitment has paid off. Today Stephanie is married and God has given her a beautiful little girl. She and her husband serve the Lord faithfully. She builds new towers of truth as she meditates on the Scriptures day by day, and God has truly set her free.

WHAT IS BONDAGE?

In many cases, though, the strength of the flesh is powerful. We can't achieve freedom because Satan has "bound us." What is this bondage that can so destroy our lives?

Bondage is living in a state of servitude to and dependence on someone or something else. The individual can't freely enjoy life in Jesus Christ because his sin encloses him and walls off the Lord's love and power. Bondage means living according to the flesh, being captivated or misdirected by the lies of the enemy, or falling in love with the present world system. For instance, one symptom is to be so absorbed and enamored with the world that your self-interests replace any level of devotion to God. This is characterized by willfulness, desiring your own way, giving in to the lusts of the flesh, and even religiously performing to improve your self-esteem rather than obeying God. Performing for others only pleases ourselves. But obedience glorifies God.

THE INIQUITIES OF OUR FATHERS

Through this process, one of the first steps toward freedom is acknowledging the iniquities of our fathers. This is a biblical command ordered in Leviticus 26:40, 42 and first given in the Ten Commandments (see Exodus 20:5–6 and 34:7). I believe we are to acknowledge, as did Jeremiah (Jeremiah 14:20), Daniel (Daniel 9:4–19), and Nehemiah (Nehemiah 9:2–37), that we are linked to the iniquities of our fathers.

The Scriptures give many examples of the iniquities of the fathers being passed on to the children. We see deception being passed from Abraham to Isaac to Jacob and Jacob's sons. King David passed the iniquity of immorality to his sons.

I believe there is New Testament basis for confession found in 1 John 1:9, "If we confess our sins, He is faithful and just to forgive us our sins and to cleanse us from all unrighteousness." The word unrighteousness is *adikia,* the Greek word for *iniquity.*

The Lord delights in setting us free from the influence of the sinful ground given by our generational lineage going back three and four generations. We are not guilty for their sins, but their iniquities (areas of willful self-advancement) tend to transfer to us. This willfulness becomes a problem for many because (1) we tend to imitate our parents and (2) we often justify sin by what our parents did.

What is the remedy? According to Scripture, we must:

- agree with God and repent of our own sin.
- admit our father's iniquities (Leviticus 26:40–42).
- develop resistance against these sins.

LIKE FATHER, LIKE SON

Not all willful behavior is influenced by our parents, of course. Some of us have godly parents who have themselves found freedom from the world's system. But if we see our selfish behavior being similar to that of our parents, we can suspect the iniquities of our parents as a major contributing factor to our behavior.

In all the warfare counseling I have done, no subject comes under fire like the issue of the iniquities of the fathers. This happened in one family who came in for counseling.

Harold, age eleven, and his father walked into my office one day. The dad said, "We as father and son have a problem. I have an anger problem and my son has the same. Part of it was probably learned from me, but I think part was passed on through my iniquities."

After we talked I could see that there was clearly a predisposition toward anger in his life. On the basis of Scripture, I believe that the iniquities of the fathers (or mothers) in an area of weakness have a spiritual dimension that is perhaps greater than we can imagine. In Harold's case, I learned this anger problem had come from past generations as well. Thus, I had dad and son acknowledge the iniquities of their fathers to the third and fourth generation and ask God by the power of His Holy Spirit to break off the influence and power of those iniquities.

Months later, Harold told me that from that day on he had a whole new level of control over his temper. His mother even said that he would do the laundry without becoming angry toward her. When it comes to eleven-year-old boys, frankly, I can't think of a stronger testimony!

I encourage you to search the Scriptures to see what God says concerning the iniquities of the parents. Ask the Holy Spirit to illumine the Word of God and see if there are some areas that perhaps need to be dealt with in your own life. It's a reality that we all must deal with to some degree, especially if serious problems have passed on for years.

WHAT IS FREEDOM?

What then is the freedom we seek?

It's the ability to live our lives in obedience to the Holy Spirit. The enemy's plan is to lie to us to get us to live in our power and desires—to live in the flesh. Living life this way leads only to more sin. This actually renders the believer entirely incapable of advancing the kingdom of God. Satan loves that.

In contrast, Jesus offers us truth and grace, the two spiritual realities that lead to freedom. Truth is the direction God desires to take us, and grace is the means He uses to get us there.

I saw this in the case of Shelton. He came to my office moderately depressed, and surely mentally tormented. He had met his wife nine years before, after they had corresponded for a year by mail. Shelton knew from this that there had been one sexual relationship in Susan's background. It was not an issue for him; it took place before they were married and it did not bother him that she did not come to the marriage bed a virgin.

Both of them had been saved about the same time. So for eight years their marriage had been blissful. The Lord gave them three children. However, Susan came under conviction that she needed to clear the air concerning some past issues. She finally told him that there was not simply one relationship but several dozen intimate relationships before she had met Shelton. Upon this admission, the enemy stole in and played upon Shelton's hurt and fear that followed the revelation. "You did not marry a wife; you married a prostitute," Shelton told himself.

Although he knew all those relationships had been forgiven by Jesus Christ, Shelton still lived in a state of sheer mental torment. He said, "I can't even stand to look at her. If it were not for the children, I would divorce her."

I knew that I was dealing with a problem where quoting Scripture would not be meaningful because the emotional baggage and trauma that he carried was overwhelming his thinking. So I said, "Let's pray."

I began to cry out to God and said, "Concerning your dear wife, I am going to ask God the truth about her. Is she a prostitute or a forgiven woman?"

In a matter of seconds, the Holy Spirit spoke to Shelton's heart and said, "She is pure by My [Christ's] blood."

Then Shelton sensed the Lord saying, "But you have become defiled by not accepting what God has declared as clean. You have allowed the enemy to defile your own heart." Shelton's extremely harsh judgment of his wife's actions before salvation had inflicted such bitterness on his soul that he was actually destroying himself.

As I prayed and then Shelton prayed, God uniquely brought His grace and truth into Shelton's heart. He cried out to God to help him forgive his wife and release her and to allow the peace and joy of God to replace the bitterness and torment in his heart. God did exactly that. Through his tears, Shelton said, "I think God has released me and my wife from our sin!"

Shelton went home that day and embraced Susan, asked her forgiveness, and they both had a quiet night of restoration, redemption, and love.

I believe God salvaged their marriage that day in the office. God used truth to take Shelton where He wanted him to go, and He used grace as a means to get him there.

That day the enemy lost a key battle.

RETURNING TO GRACE AND TRUTH . . .

The great deceiver ultimately wants to rob us of the power of grace and truth in our lives. Thus, he attacks our minds and emotions, looking for a place in our lives where he might gain a foothold. For instance, he will pressure us to become proud about certain accomplishments, talents, or physical aspects of our bodies. This pride opens the door to an attack on individual problems and practices that don't please God, such as prejudice, hatred, anger, jealousy, envy, lust, and numerous other things. Because of pride, we refuse to acknowledge the sin, and because of the sin we lose our reputation and perhaps even our careers, marriages, and so forth. It's then people come to me and say, "Please fix it!"

To "fix it," I have to go back to the bedrock problems that started the whole thing, then lead them to confess their pride, repair their character and make restitution for their sins. For many people, this is difficult to the point that they rail in anger at me, saying there has to be another way.

. . . FROM PRIDE AND BITTERNESS

In robbing us of grace and truth, the Evil One uses a bitter heart as easily as he uses a proud one. In 1979, during my first pastorate, I was called to the bedside of an old man I'll call Nelson. He claimed to have made a profession of faith as a young man, and he attended all the services of the church. But Nelson had the reputation of being the most bitter man in town.

Nelson was dying, and the doctor said he would not live through the night. When I approached his bed in the intensive care unit, he called me over to his side and said, "Let me tell you about my no-good, worthless, rotten brother-in-law."

I listened sadly as the story spilled out.

"In 1929 I had a brand-new Model A Ford car. Back in those days we did not use antifreeze, we used alcohol. Being in a northern state, it was the fall of that year when we needed it. Alcohol was expensive, so I put water in the radiator until I could afford the alcohol. My brother-in-law wanted to borrow the car. I asked him to drain not only the radiator but also the engine block when he finished driving that night (he was taking the car home), because if it froze it would crack the block.

"That worthless, no-good brother-in-law drained the radiator, but he did not drain the block because he was too lazy. It froze that night and cracked the block. He brought that new car back to me with the block leaking, laughed about it, and would not pay to have it welded."

His brother had been unfair and perhaps mean-spirited, but I was astonished that this event, which had happened fifty years earlier, was the cause of all his bitterness. Yet as he told that story, the bitterness reeked from him like some just-released poison gas. For fifty years, his hatred and anger had consumed him.

At that time, my understanding of warfare was next to nothing. But I did do this: I asked him to please consider forgiving his brother-in-law.

He refused, and to the best of my knowledge I don't believe he did before he died.

Now you might say, "What does this have to do with warfare?" Bitterness can burn in a person's soul for fifty years. Something that should have been forgiven the day it happened, something that cost many dollars to repair, and eventually meant a car in the junkyard for ages—something that really did not matter in an ultimate sense—had become a source of bitterness that destroyed the joy of a man's life for fifty years. In warfare, the enemy does not care what it takes to get our focus off of Jesus. He uses whatever works for his evil purpose; in this case all it took was a frozen engine block.

I plead with you: If you are bitter toward anyone on earth—forgive that person. Release him or her to the Lord. Ask God to forgive you of your bitterness and unforgiveness. Ask God to take back the ground you have given to the enemy and allow the Lord Jesus Christ to set you free. It's the only way. But it will work miracles in your own soul if you do it!

SATAN'S ATTACKS ON MEN AND WOMEN

Being aware of the enemy's devices is paramount here, but we must also reckon with the fact that God has created men and women differently. Satan often attacks men and women in notably different ways. In general, he attacks men in their thinking and women in their hearts.

More specifically, he tends to attack a man by telling him, "If you will do this (adultery, lust, anger, etc.), you will get this (nice feelings, happiness, fulfillment, etc.)." For instance, a man may get involved with pornography, drugs, and other sinful activities because he believes they will lead to short-lived "good" feelings (the pleasure of sin for a season).

In contrast, Satan often attacks a woman in her feelings initially, arousing love or compassion or hope and then leading her into a sinful deed. This means she feels happiness or hope or desire, and that leads her into sin. This is precisely what happened with Eve in the Garden of Eden. She did not see eating the fruit as rebellion, but that it was "good for wisdom." She saw a positive result of the sin that would bless her and her husband.

Trevor and Priscilla illustrated the difference during their counseling sessions. They wanted to speak with me individually concerning their marriage problems, so I simply said, "Ladies first."

Priscilla came in and, after getting acquainted, she said, "Let me tell you what my husband is like. This is my second marriage. My first husband was abusive to such a degree I was forced to leave him. There were no children, and we got divorced. I began looking for a man who would love me and cherish me. When I met Trevor, I thought I had found him. However, shortly after we were married I realized there was a side to him that I had never seen before. I am really wounded; I feel beat down. I feel he is constantly critical of me, and I am little more than a slave to him. He barks orders at me and the children. He is very difficult to live with."

"What do you do to deal with this pain in your life?" I asked.

After staring at the floor for a while, she said, "Well, I spend a lot of time with soap operas and romance novels, and I talk a great deal about this to my female friends."

I said, walking on what might be thin ice, "Then occasionally you have a pity party."

She said, "My life is one big pity party."

I dismissed Priscilla and invited Trevor to come in. Again we got acquainted and I said, "Trevor, what's happening?"

He said, "My marriage is on the rocks. This is my third wife. I can't understand it. It seems to happen every time I am married. I guess I just have bad luck when it comes to picking wives. She is cold to me and indifferent. When we were first married she did some housekeeping and cooked some decent meals, but now I have to yell at her to get her to do anything. We haven't been intimate in months. She sleeps in a different bedroom."

"What do you do to deal with your pain in the midst of this?"

"Well, I have been down at the bar some, spent a lot of time at the shop," he answered. "Far more time than I should has been spent with pornography."

"Uh-huh," I said.

None of this was too amazing to me when it comes to warfare. It shows how a man and a woman respond differently to the same struggles. Priscilla turned inward when he was attacking her heart and her emotions. Trevor turned outward to her rejection and used drinking and pornography as his "aspirin."

Their rebellion against God showed up in fantasizing, indulging in sin, and ignoring God's Word. The answer in this situation was repentance: Priscilla needed to repent for not fulfilling her biblical

duty in respecting her husband; Trevor needed to repent for not fulfilling his biblical duty to love his wife.

We went into much detail about these things and what the Scriptures had to say about them. Gradually, God took back the ground
they had given to Satan, and the Holy Spirit brought grace into their
life. Trevor recently told me they had taken a four-week vacation away
from work, neighbors, and the children. He said, "My wife and I
have never been so close in our lives. God is healing our marriage."

Although men and women respond differently to the same problems, the answers remain the same: seeking God, repenting, obeying
His principles about your situation, and beginning a renewed walk
with Him. I'm always amazed that often it seems just that simple.
What is not simple is finding the specific principles that deal with
your circumstance. But that's my job. If counselees will follow God's
way, I can almost always guarantee new freedom and health will come
into their lives for good.

OVERCOMING THE ENEMY'S LIES

Sometimes Christians know the source of true freedom, but cannot apply it because of sins of parents or others that leave lasting
wounds. What can they do? Arnold grew up with an angry, alcoholic father. Though he longed to bond to his father, all he received
was neglect, criticism, verbal mistreatment, and physical abuse. Arnold
remembered at age seventeen standing in the kitchen and in total frustration screaming at his father, "I can never please you, no matter how
hard I try. No matter what I do, it's never good enough!"

Years of abuse, neglect, and criticism took a toll. At age thirty,
Arnold would weep uncontrollably every time he made a mistake.
Often, when he "flubbed up," he would hear the echo of his father's
voice in his heart: "You stupid idiot, you can't do nothing right."

When Arnold was young, his father followed such devastating
words with the sting of a belt or the bash of a fist. Just recalling the
memory in my office caused Arnold to shake all over. The tears would
then stream down his face. He told me that over the years he had been
unable to hold down a job, the fear of failing so paralyzed him.

Despite these setbacks, Arnold was sensitive and intelligent. He accepted the Lord at a young age. His mother was a quiet Christian woman who stayed with her husband despite his abuse. She suffered as much as her son and put up with other sins, like infidelity. His mother told me she remembered Arnold's father becoming angry when Arnold was one year old. The boy began crying for long periods. One day after slapping Arnold several times, his father threw him and his car seat across the yard.

I spoke to Arnold gently of his need to trust the Lord, but that became a major hurdle. He said, "If God couldn't set things right when I was a child, how can I trust Him with anything now?"

After thirty minutes of weeping during our first session, Arnold calmed down enough so he and I could pray.

The amazing thing here was that not only was Arnold a believer, but he had also served in a Christian ministry before becoming totally dysfunctional and unemployable because of his depression and despair. Two years ago he decided he could no longer wall off the awful memories of his past. Several people encouraged him to seek counseling. By the time he came to our office he was desperate to find real freedom—to live, to work, to give.

To find real freedom, Arnold did what many must do: He forgave his dad. I could see the struggle on his face when he knew he must do so. Finally, bowing his head and shaking with grief, he forgave his dad. In tears, he released the pain and offenses to the Lord. He asked the Lord to take back the ground given up by his bitterness, anger, and lack of forgiveness. "God, please forgive me, my dad, all of us!"

This became the beginning of a process in which the Lord revealed deep-seated lies in Arnold's heart. As we prayed, the Lord began to speak to Arnold in a still small voice. In the end, God revealed to Arnold nineteen lies he was believing, everything from "sex is dirty" to "you are hopeless; God can't help you."

Nineteen lies! They were piled there in his heart like so many logs on a bonfire that consumed him with anger, depression, and despair. As we dealt with each of those lies, though, Arnold found real freedom and praises God today. As he continues to renew his mind in the Scriptures, the remaining pain and bondage of the past leaves daily. Again, true freedom often means forgiving those who have hurt and offended you.

HOW TO PERSEVERE IN FREEDOM

Why do good, God-loving people like Arnold fall to such lies? Among the major reasons people fail, two stand out. First, people overestimate themselves, and second, they underestimate sin. Treating sin like sin treats us offers a primary answer. Sin seeks to destroy us. Thus, we must let the Spirit of God destroy it in our lives.

A female friend of mine struggled with evil thoughts and feelings. Her mother took her to a Christian counselor who told my twenty-five-year-old friend, "You need to masturbate to release your sexual frustrations." When my friend responded, "It is not God's plan and the Scriptures tell me to control lust rather than seek self-gratification," the counselor replied, "It's all under the blood." This counselor also recommended that Carla use pornography to overcome her problem with "uptightness about modesty."

I do not mean to deride this Christian counselor, but he was not employing biblical counseling. It was more a kind of "common sense" or actually "worldly sense" of counseling. God's truth must replace such lies.

When Carla asked me about such counsel, I told her, "Carla, you need to thank God that you are a female and that God gave you sexual feelings, that He created those for a purpose. God will give you grace to keep those feelings under control. All masturbation is going to do is create more sexual frustration. I believe the Lord has given us some instructions in Romans 6:1–2: 'What shall we say then? Shall we continue in sin that grace may abound? Certainly not! How shall we who died to sin live any longer in it?'"

I went on to explain that part of her problem about modesty was not that she was so uptight but that we live in a society that is so loose. I said, "Our culture has become casual and somewhat shameless, and strands of this disease have spread out into the church. So, the thing to do is to dress in a way that is most comfortable to you, as long as that does not mean wearing several layers of clothing."

Sometimes a person like Carla needs to think through these issues scripturally. After our visit, she returned home, and the last report that I received was that she was stable, working a full-time job, and serving the Lord. These issues are no longer major problems in her life.

Once again, the only antidote to Satan's lies is God's truth. Those who counsel, whether professionally or just as Christian friends talking over coffee, must rely on Him who is the truth and His Word, for only that truth can set them free.

CHAPTER TWENTY

HOW
TO GET
TRUE
FREEDOM

*F*ear. *Freedom.* Two words could not be more opposite. Nor could the sources of each be more opposite. Fear comes from the Evil One, and he creates panic through fear. In contrast, God gives us the Holy Spirit, whose presence replaces fear. He also gives us power and love. Because of this power, we can freely choose thoughts that are victorious, loving, and right.

Paul expressed it well: "For God has not given us a spirit of fear, but of power and of love and of a sound mind" (2 Timothy 1:7).

FEARS SATAN USES

Satan's lies often appeal to our fears. One of the greatest fears Satan inflicts us with is the fear of rejection. God shows us in His Word that this fear is unfounded and something we can easily deal with if we choose.

Pearl has a solid marriage and several children, all of whom she teaches at home. This homeschooling mom has tough but fair standards for her children and won't allow them to participate in certain activities. Some neighbors are surprised and critical of Pearl's regulations for her children, and she admits their criticism makes her insecure and doubtful of her approach.

"Some people think I'm too tough," Pearl told me one day. "This whole thing that 'the fear of man brings a snare' is very powerful in my life," she said, referring to Proverbs 29:25. "I would cringe every time someone criticized my children or how I was living. Some time ago the Lord brought that verse to me, that the fear of man brings a snare. For a whole year that verse would come to my mind, and every day I would ponder it and meditate on it."

Meditating on Scripture is an excellent way to absorb the truth. It helped Pearl greatly, until one day she realized its impact. She returned to me with a smile of victory. "One day this person made a very critical statement about my family. I had no negative reactions at all. My thought was 'the fear of man brings a snare.' That critical remark was that lady's opinion; it does not happen to be mine. I was able to thank the Lord that the truth had gotten to my heart."

Pearl learned a great principle: Overturn Satan's fear tactics with the truth. We will look at this shortly. But keep in mind that Satan has other fear tactics besides the criticism of others by which he tries to undo a Christian's freedom. Beyond rejection, Satan often engenders fears related to worry or guilt about something wrong when our actions were not wrong. He will also stir up others to accuse us of wrongful things we have not done. These kinds of brutal condemnation can deeply wound us.

FACING ACCUSATIONS AND CONDEMNATION WITH THE TRUTH

What should we do when accused? Tell the enemy to "take it up with Jesus." He died for our sins and any wrongs we might have committed. Thus, we can go our way knowing He will deal with the devil. It's when we dwell on those accusations that we begin to slip.

Such accusations were a part of Rodney's life recently, and this is how he handled it.

Rodney is involved in a major Christian ministry that has a world-wide reputation. Someone involved in a branch of that ministry began to question Rodney's motives and actions publicly. Often, he would take some of Rodney's statements out of context and use them as weapons against him. There were phone calls and letters written, but even when Rodney's critic was faced with facts and documentation, it didn't matter. Things would start all over again with new "facts." Rodney would graciously answer the critic, but he came to the point of saying, like David of Shimei, "God has allowed him to curse; let him curse" (see 2 Samuel 16:11).

Rodney said to me, "God's grace is sufficient. No weapon against me will flourish without God's permission. I will leave it with the Lord."

As Rodney continued to read the Scriptures, the Lord took him to Psalm 37, which describes God blessing those who are criticized and hated. The more his critic would curse him, the more God would bless. God can turn a curse into a blessing every time, if we will let Him.

THE TRUTH WILL DRIVE OUT DECEPTION

What if the accusations are true, though? What if what Satan is saying is right? For sometimes he does say what's true. "You hurt so and so." Or, "You sinned in such-and-such a manner." What do we do then?

It always comes back to the same principle: "The truth shall make you free" (John 8:32). Admit the truth, confess the sin, and go on. If restitution is necessary, provide it. Otherwise, leave it in the hands of God. It's really as simple as that.

How can we walk in the freedom Christ won for us at Calvary? Here are three truths about our relationship with God we can count on.

1. *The Power Not to Sin.* First, as the redeemed, we do not have to sin. As God's new creation, we can walk by the Spirit, and He gives us control over the flesh. All of our sin (past, present, and future) is forgiven (Colossians 2:13). Now God can have an intimate love relationship with us as His redeemed ones. There

is no more separation between God and redeemed man (even though God is still God and man is still man). In fact, God lives in union with the believer. God has declared us to be holy, irreproachable, blameless, complete in Christ, and fit for heaven.

2. *Protection.* As redeemed children, God the Father promises us protection from the enemy. We read, "We know that whoever is born of God does not sin; but he who has been born of God keeps himself, and the wicked one does not touch him" (1 John 5:18). The Lord Jesus guards the believer who walks with Him so that the enemy will not take hold of the believer and drag him off into sin. Though we will at times fall into sin, we will not abide in it. In fact, the verb form for *sin* in 1 John 5:18 means to continue or remain in sin. If we have been born again of God, we know Satan cannot directly or continually drag us into sin. God's protection assures us. And while the spiritual battle is underway, we know God's superior might will protect us from Satan's overpowering us, "because He who is in you is greater than he who is in the world" (1 John 4:4).

3. *Comfort.* God provides comfort when we are suffering. Have you noticed how in a time of crisis the enemy will send "Job's friends" to pitch their tents in your backyard? In some cases their unsolicited "comfort" can be worse than the trial you are going through. (To see these three theologically incorrect "comforters" in action, read, for example, Job 5, 8, and 11. To see their error and God's response, read Job 42:7–9.) The true God of comfort sends true comforters who "bear one another's burdens, and so fulfill the law of Christ" (Galatians 6:2).

THE CONSOLATION OF COMFORT

I have friends who went through a tragedy that shows the kind of comfort God gives. This couple learned that their son, at age four, had atrophy of the brain and was going to die. Several people said to them, "You must have done something awful for the Lord to do this to you."

Yes, people—even Christians—will say things like that.

These kind folks, though, had one friend who saw them through this very difficult time, a sweet grandmother in the church who would sit on the couch with them and weep with them. She never had to whisper a word; her tears said it all. Her tears said, "I love you, I weep when you weep, and I am here for you."

I believe that was Jesus' way of comforting these folks and helping them hang in there when so much was going wrong. Truly, He does comfort us with His unique comfort at such times.

PROMISES FOR THE BATTLE

What, then, has God promised us that ensures that we will not only gain freedom in Christ but also walk in that freedom day by day? Here are six promises God gives to those who follow Him.

PROMISE ONE: Blessings

First, God promises us His blessings. Two specific ones described in Scripture are worth mention. First, He gives us "every spiritual blessing in the heavenly places" (Ephesians 1:3). In addition to our salvation and a place in heaven, those spiritual blessings include our freedom in Christ and the fruit of the Spirit that come as we abide in Him and serve Him. Second, there is the special blessing that comes by meditating on the Word of God. The one who learns about Him and His plan—the one who has "his delight . . . in the law of the Lord, and in [that] law . . . meditates day and night"—is blessed (see Psalm 1:1–3, especially verse 2).

But these blessings do not come without cost. For instance, we can be certain that when God opens the windows of heaven to bless, Satan will open the gates of hell to blast (Revelation 2:9–10). The lost man's greatest terror is God, but God is the Christian's greatest joy. The best measure of our spiritual life is not its ecstasies, but our obedience. When we obey, we invite Satan's wrath, but God's blessings will always overcome it.

Caroline looked at me from the chair she was sitting in and said, "I have a major problem. Every time I start walking the Christian life the gates of hell open up, and the enemy himself fires his darts at me. Ken, what do I do?"

"Caroline, you're experiencing the Christian life," I said. "If the enemy can keep you defeated, if the enemy can keep you a prisoner of war, he will just leave you there. If you are not doing damage to his kingdom, your testimony is not going to get anybody saved. If you're not raising your children in such a way that they will see Christ and have a desire to walk with Him, then the Evil One will back off. He could care less about you. But when you start taking steps with the Lord as you just described, you invite the blasts of the enemy. It might seem difficult at first, but if you keep walking, you will find that Jesus Christ will walk with you. He will teach you how to fight the good fight. You will see fruit and blessing in your life."

Caroline began to understand that this life is battle; this life is warfare. I encouraged her and said, "Many Christians go from the cradle to the grave and never comprehend. Heaven is over yonder; the battle is here today. The Lord has told us to fight the good fight because we do it in His strength. I assure you, He will be with you every step of the way."

I am happy to report today that Caroline is in the battle. She is walking with the Lord, her life is being used of God, and she is doing tremendous damage to Satan's kingdom.

PROMISE TWO: The Ability to Do His Work

God's second promise is to empower us for His work. Paul expressed this truth twice in his letter to the Philippians: "God ... works in you both to will and to do for His good pleasure" and "I can do all things through Christ who strengthens me" (2:13; 4:13).

Ultimately, what is the goal of freedom in our lives? To do God's work, especially in soul winning. God will strengthen us for each work.

In the arena of winning people to faith in Christ, the average person doesn't care about how much you know until they've seen how much you care. Part of our walking in freedom is our obedience to the Lord in serving others by showing such love and care.

A man in his mid-thirties, Leroy gave me the following testimony. "I work at a tire manufacturing plant and there are several fellows there who are Christians. They were kind to me and nice even when I occasionally pulled a trick on them. They would just laugh and become part of the joke. They kept inviting me to church. One morning I showed up. They invited me to sit with them, and then one of them invited me to come home with his family after church for lunch. They just simply cared about me. I continued to go to church because of the love, care, and concern of the people. It was not the preaching, it was not the music. It was the love that was displayed to me that drew me to Jesus Christ. One day under conviction of sin I trusted Christ as my Savior."

Every church should have this testimony. We have the tendency to think that it is the music, or the preaching, or the fellowship dinners that draw people. But it is the love of Christians that draws people. The writer John said we would be known by our love. The question to ask yourself is "Are you known by your love?"

PROMISE THREE: Wisdom

"If any of you lacks wisdom, let him ask of God, who gives to all liberally and without reproach, and it will be given to him," the Scripture declares (James 1:5). Our walk in freedom is a wisdom walk. In times of trial or testing, we need spiritual wisdom.

We will love and support and give our lives to what we treasure most. In effect, we should not give our passion and commitment to anything that we cannot take to heaven with us.

Once a doctor told me that he had just sold the family home. I knew that Elvin was about to retire; I also knew that his wife and he had three grandchildren who probably would love to visit. So I asked, "How come you sold such a lovely home?"

"Who needs a 5,000-square-foot home when we're going to be traveling a great deal abroad?" he answered.

I said, "Well, that's nice. You and your wife can do some traveling."

"Yes," Elvin told me, and then he dropped his bomb. "Myra and I are committed to spending six months out of each year on the mission field. As a retiring physician, the mission agency will still let me do surgery. If they have no one for me to operate on, my hands work real well, and they can work a shovel and I can lay cement blocks and whatever else needs to be done. We are committed for the rest of our lives to serving the Lord Jesus Christ."

I was amazed but also pleased to hear that in an age when retirement is often the very goal that people strive for, work for, and save for, here was a husband-and-wife team who wanted to give those golden years to the Lord Jesus Christ to advance His kingdom. Oh, may people of this kind of character increase!

PROMISE FOUR: Peace

"Peace I leave with you, My peace I give to you" (John 14:27). During the time of storm, God's peace, "which surpasses all understanding" (Philippians 4:7), will sustain us on the inside as the waves beat on the outside.

We must bother the Lord about everything or in time everything will bother us. That is exactly what the enemy wants. An agitated and uneasy saint (without peace) is targeted for a fall. Both meditation on who He is (consulting the Scriptures) and prayer give such peace.

True, prayer can be work. Perhaps that is why we are so reluctant to exercise it. But not only is prayer work, it is the greatest work. It gives us peace, and it moves the hand of God on our behalf. This leads to God's fifth promise.

PROMISE FIVE: Answers to Prayer

God will hear and answer prayers of those who seek His help (though not always as we expect or even prefer). Jesus' commands in Matthew 7:7–9 are instructive. The three verbs that concern our prayer life are *ask, seek,* and *knock.* All are in a verb form indicating action that is continuing. In other words, "keep asking, seeking, and knocking."

In verse 8, the Lord ensures the certainty of answers to our prayers. We are assured that He hears our prayers and answers them in His loving, fatherly way according to His perfect will. And it is our faith and trust in God that leads us to continue asking. Just as it would be an insult to knock once at someone's door and leave, so with the Lord in prayer. As the apostle James explained in his classic statement on prayer, a major reason you "do not have [is] because you do not ask" (4:2).

Let's also remember that whether we pray for others or ourselves, it must be with the right motives. James added in verse 3 that when we ask with the wrong motives, we will not receive because God is not going to help us fulfill selfish desires.

A prayerless saint is prey for the enemy. Prayer usually determines whether our problems or God's promises have our life. The devil has temporary, limited control of our world system, which is why it is in such a mess. This alone should prompt us to pray.

We ought to be so familiar with prayer that the moment the enemy shows up, our response is to call upon the Lord for help (Psalm 50:15; 91:15).

When the enemy shows up, resist him and cry out to God. There is no better prescription for dealing with temptation.

PROMISE SIX: Help Against Temptation

"No temptation has overtaken you except such as is common to man; but God is faithful, who will not allow you to be tempted beyond what you are able, but with the temptation will also make the way of escape, that you may be able to bear it" (1 Corinthians 10:13). These words offer encouragement and assurance that it is not necessary that we fall as the Israelites did in the earlier verses of this chapter (6–10). This is a call for us to learn from the Old Testament examples. From these we learn God is with us and He will strengthen us and help us stand.

The temptation spoken of in verse 13 has two important aspects to it: (1) any temptation to sin comes from the enemy, never from God; and (2) it's a testing that God allows for the purpose of our refinement and purification.

Through the Lord's strength we can bear the temptation and pass the test. He is not the originator of the temptation, but He is in control of the temptation. He is always available to help us through the temptation. He not only limits the temptation, but in His sovereignty supplies the means of escape. Thus, we are assured that in His perfect timing the Lord will remove the trial.

WAR WITHOUT FEAR

Today, you are at the end of this book. You have read many pages trying to understand and prepare for the battle that swirls around you. I hope I have shown you convincingly that this battle is reality.

But it's also my hope that you are no longer uninformed or weaponless or afraid. The victory is assured. Christ has won it. We need only begin mop-up operations to drive the devil out of the few lone bastions where he uses lies and deceit to make us think he has a right to be there.

He doesn't.

And you are the key. Wage war without fear, without worry, without despair. Your Lord is at your right hand; His Word in your left. The armor is on your body, and the Spirit is in your heart. The church stands ready to assist, and should you fall and become confused, others like myself can step in and disband the darkness.

All the resources are there. You need nothing else. Go; walk in the freedom Christ has given you.

To Him be the glory!

1. Are you free in Christ?

2. How does Satan usually trip you up?

3. Do you read the Word daily?

NOTES

Chapter 7: Jesus Is a Faithful Friend

1. The weight of New Testament evidence shows that divorce and remarriage are prohibited (Matthew 19:3–12; Mark 10:2–9; Luke 16:10; Romans 7:1–3; 1 Corinthians 7:10–16, etc. To those who are already remarried: Nowhere does God command spouses to separate and live as single people. The Scriptures do treat second marraiges as having significant standing in God's eyes. Vows were made and a union was formed. Those promises are to be kept, and the marriage is to be sanctified to God.

Chapter 8: The Power of the Truth

1. Martha found special help from five concepts of God's acceptance and good plans: (1) God fully accepts me in Christ (Ephesians 1:6); (2) God is trustworthy (Proverbs 3:5–6; Isaiah 28:16); (3) God has never and will never make a mistake (Isaiah 46:10); (4) God will always give me grace that is sufficient for the hour (1 Corinthians 10:13; 2 Corinthians 12:9); and (5) God will cause everything that has happened to work for His glory and my good (Genesis 50:20; Romans 8:28–29).

Chapter 10: More Essential Equipment

1. Warren Wiersbe, *The Strategy of Satan* (Wheaton, Ill.: Tyndale, 1985), 83.

Chapter 15: When Your Church Becomes Infected

1. I have visited with Apostle Smith on two occasions. He in no way comes across as a fluke or a charlatan. I honestly believe he is a deceived deceiver. He believes there are many empowered churches worldwide, but they must be under the authority of a "true" apostle to have that authority. Apostle Smith says, "Put things in divine order and the power will flow through the apostle down to the prophets, evangelists, pastors, and teachers to the people." Whether by intent or accident, this "apostle" is being used by Satan to deceive those in Christ's church.

Chapter 16: The Power of Prayer, Love, and Compassion

1. Details of this story were compiled through interviews with the senior pastor, associate pastor, and members of this Baptist church during several visits.

Chapter 17: The Wounds of Abuse

1. Henry T. Blackaby & Claude V. King, *Experiencing God* (Nashville: Lifeway, 1990), 76, 89, 130.
2. Ibid., 160.

Chapter 18: Help and Healing from the Great Physician

1. If you or a friend has experienced occult abuse, God may deal directly, as He did with Daisy's learning through her baby-sitter about Bible studies. At other times, you may need to seek pastoral counsel or other professional help. Though God may not intervene directly, He is involved and He does care.

Moody Press, a ministry of Moody Bible Institute,
is designed for education, evangelization, and edification.
If we may assist you in knowing more about Christ
and the Christian life, please write us without obligation:
Moody Press, c/o MLM, Chicago, Illinois 60610.